The Sense of Quality

BERNARD BERENSON

The Sense of Quality

STUDY AND CRITICISM OF ITALIAN ART

SCHOCKEN BOOKS · NEW YORK

THE STUDY AND CRITICISM
OF ITALIAN ART * FIRST SERIES

First SCHOCKEN PAPERBACK edition 1962

Library of Congress Catalog Card No. 62-19394

Manufactured in the United States of America

PREFACE

THE papers republished in this volume have appeared
at various times during the last ten years. Some of
them, like those, for instance, on Correggio, were
written two or three years before they were printed.
These particularly I cannot present in the more
pretentious form of a book without a word of apology.

Few will be more convinced of their crudity and
their juvenility than I am. Yet they show signs of
striving towards a critical method. In the first it is
crassly Morellian, redeemed only, for me at least,
by a touch of glamour, of the innocent illusion which
in another form makes so many simple-minded
people who have failed to find an æsthetic gospel
in Ruskin, imagine a vain thing, and seek for it in
the sterile prosings of the so-called connoisseurs. I
see now how fruitless an interest is the history of
art, and how worthless an undertaking is that of
determining who painted, or carved, or built whatsoever it be. I see now how valueless all such
matters are in the life of the spirit. But as, at the
same time, I see more clearly than ever that without
connoisseurship a history of art is impossible, and
as my readers presumably are to be students of this
history, many of them in the aspiring state of mind

v

that I then was in, I feel a certain justification in
laying before them this juvenile essay. Moreover,
although written more than ten years ago, I must
already have known Correggio better than most
other writers ; for, as will be seen, I did not hesitate
therein to assign to that master's youth a work then
almost unknown, and not recognized as his, that
"Adoration of the Magi," which recently, as a now
universally accepted Correggio, has been transferred
from the Archiepiscopal Palace of Milan to the Brera.
I attempted also to work out the story of the artist's
genesis, as it had not yet been done, and as, to my
knowledge, it has not been done since. The question,
for instance, of his indebtedness to Dosso deserves at
least all the consideration I gave it. Finally, not
my least excuse for this paper is that it contains the
one attempt, in English at least, to give an adequate
characterization of this fascinating and romantic, if
provincial, and slovenly Ferrarese painter.

The second paper on Correggio was written a year
or two later, and in a vague, groping way, suggests
a method of studying an artist which, when based on
an impeccable connoisseurship, must enable us to
define his artistic personality, and account for his
failures as well as successes. To the layman this
certainly is a more promising problem than the mere
determination of authorship, yet even this will profit
him but little if his purpose be what it should be—
to enjoy the kernel of the work of art, shelled of all
the husks of historical, literary, and personal consideration.

But even the history of art should be studied much

more abstractly than it has ever been studied, and
freed as much as possible from entangling irrelevan-
cies of personal anecdote and parasitic growths of
petty documentation. The still prevalent way of
study is the stupid inheritance of a past when people
who had done life's tasks, or had not the brains to do
them, and such people only, dribbled away their useless hours on making the darkness which enveloped
art foolishly visible. And now it is continued out
of bad habit, and still more out of an itch for work
on the part of beings too lazy or too ungifted to use
their minds. I am among the first to question the
spiritual value of art history, yet to be well done, it
also requires an intelligence of no mean order, tact
and judgment of the first kind, and an industrious-
ness immeasurably more of the mind than of the
reading eye or copying hand. I, for one, have been
for many years cherishing the conviction that the
world's art can be, nay, should be, studied as inde-
pendently of all documents as is the world's fauna
or the world's flora. The effort to classify the one
should proceed along the line of the others, and if
done with equal brains and equal strenuousness of
purpose, the success surely should be equal. Such
a classification would yield material not only ample
enough for the universal history of art, but precise
enough, if qualitative analysis also be applied, for
the perfect determination of purely artistic personalities. Then, and only then, and chiefly for mere
convenience of naming, might one turn to documents
—which in the meantime should be published by
carefully trained and scrupulously faithful archivists

—and attempt to connect with this abstract some actual personality of the past.

In this spirit, and with such intent did I for many years study a group of pictures which the careless classification of indifferent ages had permitted to pass for Filippo's, or Botticelli's, or Fillipino's, or even Ghirlandajo's. The result of these studies was the article on "Amico di Sandro," here reprinted. I attempted without the aid of a single document, or a single "literary" hint to construct an artistic personality; to show how it proceeded from, how it was influenced by, and how it influenced other such personalities; and even to establish with fair accuracy the period when this personality was active. All this work was done before my friend, Mr. Herbert Horne, who had been for some time following my studies with benevolent interest, came to me with the suggestion that this artistic personality might be connected with a real person.

I spoke just now of qualitative analysis as essential to the construction of any given artistic personality. With an analysis merely quantitative, we shall be able to define the motives and general ideas of a given artist, but never his most intimate *vivida vis*, his ultimate power of giving independent existence to his imaginings. Quantitative analysis such as, if you are foolish enough to take him at his word, Morelli seemed to advocate as all sufficing, is within the capacity of any serious student armed with patience and good habits of observation; but the sense of quality must first exist as God's gift, whereupon, to become effective, it should be submitted to many years of arduous training. Only the person thus gifted and trained may approach the inner shrine of the Muses, and not be overtaken by a fate worse than of Midas.

To illustrate this and kindred topics, I wrote the essay on copies after lost originals by Giorgione ; but once launched on a theme so noble, I did not hesitate to say a little of what I *felt* about this rarest, and most unattainable of painters. Let me add that were I to see the St. Petersburg "Judith" (which I know by the photograph only) I might have to acknowledge that it was an original repainted almost beyond recognition, and not a copy. This, however, would not prove my method the worse - and method interests me more than results, the functioning of the mind much more than the ephemeral object of functioning.

I must take a much humbler tone in speaking of another paper in this volume, one on the Venetian Exhibition. It was written in haste, printed at the expense of my dear friend Mr. Herbert Cook, and distributed at the exhibition itself. My excuse for reprinting it is that it contains a number of general remarks on method, and much information on Venetian pictures in England. Although I wrote in haste, I was at the time so steeped in the painting of Venice, that, while I have all along kept up my interest in Venetian art, I nevertheless find, on reading over this paper, very little to change either in general statement or in the attributions.

In a book of essays tending to illustrate a way of studying and criticising Italian art, a paper on Vasari, the one great writer on the subject, and the founder of all study concerning it, needs no apology. The too brief note on Dante's visual images I insert in the hope that some one may be found with more leisure than is mine to develop the idea to something like the fullness it demands. To him who grasps it, it should furnish the theme for a book as fascinating as it would be illuminating.

My thanks are due to the editors of the "New York Nation" and the "Gazette des Beaux Arts," for the kind permission to reprint articles that they published.

April, 1901.

CONTENTS

	PAGE
VASARI IN THE LIGHT OF RECENT PUBLICATIONS	I
DANTE'S VISUAL IMAGES, AND HIS EARLY ILLUS- TRATORS	13
SOME COMMENTS ON CORREGGIO IN CONNECTION WITH HIS PICTURES IN DRESDEN	20
THE FOURTH CENTENARY OF CORREGGIO	39
AMICO DI SANDRO	46
CERTAIN COPIES AFTER LOST ORIGINALS BY GIORGIONE	70
VENETIAN PAINTING, CHIEFLY BEFORE TITIAN, AT THE EXHIBITION OF VENETIAN ART	90
INDEX	147

LIST OF ILLUSTRATIONS

TO FACE
PAGE

AMICO DI SANDRO.
Virgin and Child with two Angels.   46
Madonna and Child with St. John.   48
Tobias and the Archangels.   50
Study for a Tobias and the Archangels.   50
The Coronation of the Virgin.   52
The Adoration of the Magi.   54
The Story of Esther.   56
Esther.   56
Madonna and Child   58
Madonna and Child.   58
Portrait of Esmeralda Bandinelli.   60
Two Angels.   60
Portrait of Giuliano de' Medici.   62
La Bella Simonetta.   62
Bust of a Youth.   64

BASAITI.
Virgin and Child with four Saints.   110

GENTILE BELLINI.
Madonna and Child.   118

BOTTICELLI.
The Chigi Madonna.   46

CARIANI.
The Concert.   140
Shepherd and Lady.   140
Holy Family and Donors.   140

CATENA.
The Nativity.   132

CIMA.
Holy Family in a Landscape   108

xiii

TO FACE
PAGE

CORREGGIO.
 The Nativity.
 Christ taking leave of his Mother.   34
 The Adoration of the Magi.   36
 The Madonna of St. Francis.   38
                                                     42

CRIVELLI.
 A Pietà.   100

GIORGIONE.
 The Finding of Paris.
 Apollo and Daphne.   74
 The Shepherd Boy.   78
                                                     142

COPIES AFTER GIORGIONE.
 David.
 Orpheus and Eurydice.   72
 Portrait of a Gentleman.   76
 Portrait of a Lady.   82
                                                     84

LICINIO.
 A Lady Professor of the University of Bologna.   138

ROCCO MARCONI (?).
 Portrait of a man.   126

BARTOLOMMEO MONTAGNA.
 Madonna and Child.   114

QUIRICO DA MURANO (?)
 St. George and the Dragon.   102

ROMANINO.
 Musicians.   136

RONDINELLI.
 Portrait of a Youth.   124

BARTOLOMMEO VENETO.
 Madonna and Child with two Angels.   134

ALVISE VIVARINI.
 Portrait of a Youth.   104

The Sense of Quality

VASARI IN THE LIGHT OF RECENT PUBLICATIONS

"THE Florentine masters," it has been said, "are the Dr. Johnsons of Art : they are so much more fascinating in the pages of their Boswell than in their own works." This illuminating paradox would lose none of its lustre, and would gain in force, if it were limited to the painters. It is certainly true that many Florentine painters who enjoy a considerable reputation because they figure in Vasari, would scarcely have roused a moment's curiosity if they had had to depend upon their works alone to awaken it. The more candidly one looks, the more inevitable this conclusion becomes, and it is more than questionable whether our interest in Vasari's "Vite" be not, after all, quite independent of the scores of second and third-rate pictures it celebrates; and whether it is not, by itself, and on its own account, one of the very greatest products of Tuscan genius.

Some such view of Vasari would account for the hold he has not only upon people who read him as literature, but upon students of the history of art. They soon discover that he is not an historian of the late Prof. Freeman's kind—in fact, that he never in his life consulted a document ; and, worse still, that he rarely made accurate use of the information he had gathered. He abounds in contradictions ; he makes long excursions on loop-lines to kick an enemy or to puff a friend ; a tenth-rate painter working under the shadow of Brunelleschi's dome is more interesting to him than a great master elsewhere—and yet one comes back to him with an ever-increasing sense of his charm and fascination. He has this charm and fascination because he wrote down with the naïveté of an Herodotus the folk-lore, romance, and gossip that had, in the course of two centuries, gathered in profusion about the artists, a class of people who in Florence formed a more prominent and more self-conscious part of the community than they did in any other Italian city. Their fellow-townsmen, therefore, took the keenest imaginable interest in them both as a class and as individuals, and heard and repeated stories about them with that delight in personal anecdote which was the distinguishing mark of the Florentine populace and of their literature. It was for such a public that Vasari wrote, and this acounts for his method and his success. He had to be personal, gossipy, and readable. His unerring sense of the readable made him arrange his material in a way that would catch the eye, no matter at what cost to mere veracity, and for that reason he succeeded where others failed.

The student of history soon learns to assume that every success in any definite line of achievement is preceded and surrounded by a great many attempts in the same direction. Even if we lacked positive information, we might be sure that Vasari was not the first nor the only Italian to write lives of painters. As a matter of fact, Vasari's publication stopped many who were at that very time occupied with the same task, as was the case, for instance, with the "Anonimo Morelliano" (probably the Venetian Michiel). In further proof of this we may cite Prof. Carl Frey's

recent publication of the materials which an unknown
Florentine contemporary of Vasari was preparing
for a history of art.[1]   The difference in spirit between
this writer and Vasari appears, however, in an
instant.   The "Anonimo Magliabecchiano" is a
scholarly compiler who gathers material from all the
books and manuscripts he can lay hold of, not only
about the artists of antiquity and of the recent past,
but about living masters.   It does not occur to him
to criticise his material, nor does he seem to have
taken the trouble to look at the works of art that he
might have seen by sticking his head out of the
window.   In fact, he mentions their works merely as
points connected with the lives of the artists, not as
the primary cause of interest in them.   Vasari, on the
contrary, always describes a picture or a statue with
the vividness of a man who saw the thing while he
wrote about it, and saw it so vividly that he did not
think of looking up his notes.   Nor does Vasari ever
forget that the capital fact in the artist's career is his
work.

But a still more striking difference between the
"Anonimo" and Vasari is that the latter clearly
realizes the difference between the ancient and the
modern world—a division which scarcely exists for
the "Anonimo."   Indeed, Vasari was one of the
first writers to feel that modern civilization was a
thing by itself, and not merely the resuscitation of a
glorious past.   Hence, in his first edition, he began
at once with Cimabue, and it was only because he
found that this shocked his contemporaries that he
prefixed, by way of introduction to his second edition,
an essay on the art of the ancients.

The modern world begins for Vasari with Cimabue,

[1] "Il Codice Magliabecchiano." Berlin : Grote'sche Verlag.
1892.

and he has a complete scheme of the growth of the arts from Cimabue to their culmination in his worshipped master, Michelangelo. That this scheme was not Vasari's invention is clearly proved by the "Anonimo," who, after he once gets to Cimabue, follows out the later history of art on much the same plan. Prof. Frey prefaces his edition of the "Anonimo" with an essay on Vasari's predecessors, in which it is established that, at the end of the fifteenth century, fifty years before Vasari wrote, the Florentines were already well aware who their great masters were. Even a generation earlier, Landino, in his Dante Commentary, gives the names of Cimabue, Giotto, Taddeo Gaddi, Masaccio, Fra Angelico, Fra Filippo, Paolo Uccello, and Andrea del Castagno, as the names of great painters no longer living; Brunelleschi, Ghiberti, Donatello, and Desiderio, as the great sculptors. Of Desiderio, Landino speaks in terms repeated not only by the "Anonimo," but, almost word for word, by Vasari himself: "And if an utterly untimely death had not snatched him away in his early years, he would have attained, as every one acquainted with the arts expected, to the utmost perfection."

A tradition of criticism can, however, be traced much further back than Landino. In a certain sense Dante himself may be looked upon as having caused the first study of Italian art. Even in the fourteenth century, his commentators had already begun to explain his reference to Cimabue and Giotto, and, in the fifteenth, the commentary on the famous lines spoken by Oderisi expanded into a sketch of the history of art from Giotto downwards. Not only in this indirect way is Dante to be considered the founder of art study, but he actually started one of the most popular art legends by his phrases "Cimabue nella pintura tener lo campo" and "ora ha Giotto il grido," thus giving an importance to Cimabue which he otherwise certainly would not have had. It is clearly proved that this, and this alone, gave rise to the elaborate romance which has made Cimabue as familiar a name as Giotto.[1]

The Cimabue legend does not, however, appear to have been at all elaborated before the end of the fifteenth century. Simultaneously with the "Anonimo Magliabecchiano," Prof. Frey has published "Il Libro di Antonio Billi," a work of the same nature, but briefer, written at different times towards the end of the fifteenth century and the first quarter of the sixteenth.[2] This note-book is of great importance, both because it shows what point the study of art had reached by the end of the fifteenth century, and because it was the common source of Vasari and the "Anonimo." The latter, being merely the crude material for a book, although already arranged in order, embodies Billi's notes unchanged, while Vasari of course adapts Billi more to his own style. It is in Billi that the story first occurs about Cimabue's Madonna being carried to Santa Maria Novella amid great rejoicing and to the sound of trumpets. Giotto's personality, on the contrary, was already fixed in the fourteenth century, and his importance fully appreciated. Boccaccio, in the "Decameron" (vi. 5), calls him "one of the glories of Florence, he who brought to light again an art buried for many centuries, and painted so wonderfully that his pictures cannot be called likenesses, for they are identical with

[1] See F. Wickhoff, "Die Zeit des Guido von Siena." Mitteilungen des Instituts für oesterreichische Geschichtsforschung. Innsbruck. Vol. X.

[2] "Il Libro di Antonio Billi." Berlin: Grote'sche Verlag. 1892.

the life, for which people mistook them." (Of course
Boccaccio himself owes his æsthetics to Pliny, who
in turn owes his to the Greeks ; but it is curious to
find him already making use of the phrase which
occurs constantly in Vasari, "pare vivo"—"seems
alive.") The same critique of Giotto is found, word
for word, both in the "Anonimo" and in his source,
Antonio Billi. The story, however, of Giotto being
discovered by Cimabue drawing sheep on a stone
occurs for the first time in Ghiberti, who wrote his
commentaries about 1450.

In fact, not only did the legends about popular
painters gather in volume with the lapse of time, but
the list of their works shared the same tendency to
expansion. Filippo Villani, for instance, speaks of
Cimabue, but mentions none of his works, nor does
Landino ; F. Alberti, writing in 1510, mentions two
or three ; Billi and the "Anonimo" cite quite a
number, while Vasari does not hesitate to attribute
to him everything "nella maniera bizantina" he can
find. It is the same with Giotto, only that in his case
the growth of the legend is directly due to the Dante
commentators. Basing themselves on the probable
fact that Giotto and Dante were acquainted, they
were on the look out for signs of the influence of
their master on his great painter-friend, and wherever
they found a face supposed to be that of Dante, as in
the Bargello Chapel, or a subject connected in the
remotest way with Hell or Purgatory, they unhesi-
tatingly ascribed the picture to Giotto. The attribution to him of the frescoes of the Bargello Chapel
can be traced back to Ghiberti, whose commentaries
had a great influence upon all later Florentine art-
historians ; but Billi is the first to attribute to Giotto
the Apocalypse in the Incoronata at Naples, adding
that it was painted, "it was said, with the help of

Dante, who, being in exile, wandered thither unknown." The "Anonimo" goes so far as to attribute
to Giotto the frescoes in the choir of Santa Croce, in-
disputably by Agnolo Gaddi, thus showing that Giotto
had, in the middle of the sixteenth century, become
almost as generic a name as "Raphael" was in the
last century.

The "Anonimo" felt that he must, if possible, connect some anecdote or startling fact with every artist;
in this, as in everything, following the lead of Pliny.
The startling fact which he connects with Orcagna,
for example, is that he was paid 86,000 ducats for his
tabernacle in Or San Michele. This is the earliest
indication of the spirit which leads the Italian sacristan
of to-day to tell us, while he is unveiling a picture,
that the Queen of England offered 500,000 francs
for it.

The good stories about Brunelleschi, told by
Vasari with sympathetic garrulity, can be traced
through the "Anonimo" and through Billi, and are
found fixed already in Manetti, who, about 1480,
wrote a life of Brunelleschi. The farther back they
are traced, however, the more do they approach the
baldness of fact. Thus Manetti has the story about
Della Luna's spoiling the Innocenti, but not Brunelleschi's retort: "There was one error in the building
of San Giovanni, and you have picked it out for a
model." Even the "Anonimo," although he speaks
of the crucifix Brunelleschi had made in rivalry with
Donatello, knows nothing of Vasari's *novella*, ending
with Donatello's ejaculation, "You were made to
carve Christs, and I clodhoppers." Billi relates that
"even a woman had dared" to offer a model for the
lantern of the cupola, but Vasari, to make it more
gossipy, adds that she belonged to the famous Gaddi
family. In one or two instances, however, Vasari

sacrifices the point of a story for ulterior purposes. Billi, for instance, relates that "Donatello was in Siena, making a door for the cathedral.   One day a goldsmith, Bernardetto di Mona Papera, happened to be passing through on his way from Rome.   He was a friend of Donatello, so he called on him, and, beholding the splendid work, he reproached him for giving the Sienese so fine a thing to boast of.   His words had such an effect that on a feast-day, when the apprentices had gone out to make holiday, Donatello and Bernadetto ruined everything, and leaving the house, took the road for Florence.   The apprentices coming home at night found everything ruined, and no Donatello ; and not a word did they hear of him until he was safe in Florence."   It would be hard to find an anecdote in which was combined to such a degree the Florentine's hatred of the Sienese and his consciousness of the splendour and glory bestowed upon a town by the works of arts within its walls. But Vasari, wishing, perhaps, to reconcile the Sienese, who, while he was writing, were being annexed to Florence, does not tell what arguments Bernardetto used with Donatello.

Poor Vasari has been most unmercifully cuffed about of late for accusing Castagno of murdering Domenico Veneziano, when, as a matter of fact, Domenico outlived Castagno.   But Vasari can no longer be blamed for inventing this calumny.   Billi relates it, and as he notes down only what he finds, the tale must have been already current at the end of the fifteenth century.   It is more than likely that the story-spinning mind of the Florentines cooked up this murder as a criticism on Castagno's works.   His energetic, gruff, almost brutal apostles and saints led to the conclusion that their painter must have been a very wicked man, just as nowadays Perugino's

sweet, dreamy, beatified faces and eternally peaceful
landscapes make it next to impossible to doubt, in
spite of positive information to the contrary, that
Perugino had an angelic nature.

Accuracy was not in the historical spirit of the sixteenth century. The "Anonimo Magliabecchiano"
is quite as inaccurate as Vasari himself. Had he
succeeded in becoming our chief source of knowledge on Italian painting, we should have been no
nearer to accuracy than we are now with Vasari as
our guide. We should simply have had another set
of grotesque theories to refute, and another set of
false attributions to put straight. To make Perugino the pupil of Botticelli, as the "Anonimo" does,
is no better than making Timoteo Viti the pupil,
instead of the master, of Raphael. Vasari, moreover,
is not guilty of anything so gross as the "Anonimo's"
attribution of Ghirlandaio's "Last Supper" in the
Ognissanti to Botticelli. This proves what has already
been said, that the "Anonimo" never looked at
pictures. The personal anecdote is his real interest,
although he has none of that narrative power and
dramatic sense which put Vasari on a level with
Boccaccio and with the best *raconteurs* of all times.
Botticelli's "crankiness," for example, interests him
more than his works, and he begins his account of
Sandro with a story not reported by Vasari:

"Tommaso Soderini was persuading him to get
married. 'I will tell you,' answered Sandro, 'what
happened a few nights ago. I dreamt I was married,
and it made me so wretched that, to avoid falling
asleep and having the dream over again, I got up,
and all night rushed about the streets of Florence
as if I were mad.' Thereupon Messer Tommaso
saw that Sandro was not the soil to plant a vine-
yard in."

In the same way, although the "Anonimo" devotes scant space to Leonardo and Michelangelo, he dwells at length upon Leonardo' beauty and personal qualities, and upon Michelangelo's bitter feeling towards his great rival. " Leonardo was passing where a number of well-to-do people were discussing a passage in Dante. They stopped him for his opinion. But Michelangelo happening to come along at that very moment, Leonardo answered : 'Michelangelo will explain it to you.' This put Michelangelo into a fury : 'Explain it yourself, you who made a model for a horse, to cast it in bronze, and could not cast it, and so let it go for shame.'" Another time he shouted to Leonardo : "So those capons of Milanese believed all you said, did they ? " (" Et che t'era creduto da que caponj de Melanesj ?") Another personal trait he recounts, bringing curious confirmation to the theory of the late Senator Morelli, that every old master had his own fixed way of painting hands : " Filippino generally made one hand larger than another, and was aware of the fault, but could not change it."

Neither Billi nor the "Anonimo" offers any fresh information. I believe the only fact of the least consequence to the history of art in either is the "Anonimo's" statement that Botticelli painted in January, 1473, a St. Sebastian that was in Santa Maria Maggiore. There is every reason to think that this St. Sebastian is the one now in Berlin, and the date is valuable as one of the few points in Sandro's career upon which to base a theory of his development.

Not only do these new documents furnish no useful supplementary information, but they are fearfully meagre as compared with Vasari, although, among modern artists, they deal with the Florentines only

They say, it is true, a few words about the Sienese *Trecentisti*, but that only because they had Ghiberti's appreciative account of the Sienese before their eyes. Otherwise, they seem utterly blind to the existence of painters outside of Florence. Signorelli and Perugini are barely mentioned, and Raphael's name does not so much as occur. How different this is from the comprehensive sweep Vasari had! To him Florence was, of course, the eye of the universe, the Florentine artists were the greatest of modern times. His "Vite" is so full of this conviction, and he has so won over his readers to it, that even to-day it sounds almost blasphemous to demur to this towering preëminence of the Florentines. Yet Vasari was an Italian as well as a Tuscan, and every artist in Italy interested him. He was a very busy man, a practising architect and a prolific painter, so he was often forced to rely on correspondents who were no less inclined to overestimate their own local painters than Vasari himself was when he spoke of any one from Arezzo. But it is not hard to distinguish these interpolations. Wherever Vasari speaks of what he has seen—and he saw nearly all the best work in Italy—and where he is not led astray by what might be called the "false morn of journalism," he is a singularly warm, generous, and appreciative critic. He feels instinctively, too, that the first function of the popular writer on art is to be interpretative. Everything considered, his interpretation is still the best there is. He is not so penetrating as Mr. Pater, nor so fantastical and poetical as Mr. Ruskin, but he is broader than either, and in closer sympathy with actual humanity. Among Italians, Vasari simply has no rival at all. Billi and the "Anonimo" make no attempt whatever at interpretation, and later writers, like Ridolfi, Baldinucci, and even Boschini, were incapable of writing down their impressions if they had any.

The chief use of the "Anonimo" and Billi is, therefore, to turn our minds to a kindlier view of Messer Giorgio. He was, to be sure, a true son of his age, and had no sense of the document. His predecessors, Billi and the "Anonimo," however, appreciate the value of documents even less. For documents we must look elsewhere. But Vasari is still the unrivalled critic of Italian art, and, regarded as literature, he was one of the great prose-writers of Italy, and the last important product of the novel-istic tendency in Tuscan genius.

DANTE'S VISUAL IMAGES, AND HIS EARLY ILLUSTRATORS

MERE learning has perhaps done its very utmost with Dante by this time, and, if that poet is not to become stagnant, his work must now be approached from other points of view, and the light of other than merely philological and philosophical erudition must be thrown upon it. Is it not rather extraordinary that thus far it has occurred to only one writer, and that not one of the corps enrolled to write on the subject, but a free-lance such as Vernon Lee, to ask the question what visual images Dante had while giving his perfectly plastic descriptions of the exterior universe? Few students of Dante stop to wonder what correspondence there can be between his visual images while writing and those called up in our minds while reading him. But those of us who visualize at all cannot read about Trajan and the Widow, let us say, without seeing an image based on someone or on a whole number of Roman bas-reliefs. Dante, however, could not have had such an acquaintance with the antique as we necessarily have, and his visual image of a scene taking place in Greece or Rome or Judea could have had no great likeness to ours. And with the figure of Virgil himself it could scarcely have been otherwise. *We* cannot help dressing Virgil as a Roman, and giving him a "classical profile" and "statuesque carriage," but Dante's visual image of Virgil was

probably no less mediæval, no more based on a
critical reconstruction of antiquity, than his entire
conception of the Roman poet. Fourteenth-century
illustrators make Virgil look like a mediæval scholar,
dressed in cap and gown, and there is no reason
why Dante's visual image of him should have been
other than this.

That Dante had visual images there can scarcely
be a doubt. We have, in proof, besides the un-
equalled plasticity of all his descriptions, the detailed
account in " Purgatorio," Canto X., of the various
reliefs representing acts of humility. These reliefs
are simply the descriptions of the visual images
called up in Dante's mind by the acts of humility.
" To take plastic shape in the mind" has become a
common phrase in criticism, but it can have no
meaning unless that of *becoming visualized;* and as
the phrase is applied to Dante, it means that Dante
visualized everything that passed through his mind.
Nothing, therefore, could bring us nearer to a knowledge of those contents of Dante's mind of which he
was himself aware while writing, than if we could
form some conception of his visual images.

Dante himself gives the clue. On the first anni-
versary of Beatrice's death, he says in the "Vita
Nuova," he sat down and drew the figure of an
angel. A student of early Tuscan art must know
how this angel looked. Dante could not have invented this figure, but, like all amateurs, he undoubtedly drew an angel of the kind his favourite
painter would have drawn, and in this instance the
painter was Giotto. Dante's angel in all likelihood
resembled one of Giotto's such as we see in Assisi,
Padua, or Florence ; and had Dante gone further
and drawn a whole scene—that is to say, exactly
rendered as only form and colour can render a visual

image—its relation to one of Giotto's whole pictures would have been the same. Dante's visual image of the Virtues, of the heavenly hosts, of Christ and the Virgin, of St. Francis, could not have been very different from Giotto's, nor even his image of Beatrice very different from one of that great painter's sleek-faced, almond-eyed, waistless women. Beatrice did not necessarily look like this. The visual image is not the direct impression of the object, but the memory of the impression more or less vague according to the varying powers of visualization ; and in a lover of the arts such as Dante was, visualization would be largely determined by the works of art with which he was intimately acquainted. It is Giotto whom Dante knew best and loved best, and it is the study of Giotto, therefore, and of kindred painters (some even closer in spirit to Dante, such as Duccio, Simone Martini, and the Lorenzetti) that will enable us to form a clear conception of Dante's visual images.

None of these painters shows trace of direct Dantesque inspiration, and none of them has left what would have been the most valuable of all commentaries on the real Dante, a series of illustrations to the " Divina Commedia." But they frequently dealt with subjects fringing on Dante's, and a systematic study of these would be a great help in reconstructing the poet's visual images. Illustrations, moreover, by their followers, the heirs of their conceptions, exist in plenty. After these contemporaries of Dante, no painter at all on a level in genius with him appeared until Signorelli, and by that time visual imagery had changed from mediæval to modern. To a certain extent the antique had already been critically reconstructed. Still, Signorelli's illustrations in the chapel of S. Brizio at Orvieto have an interest not only as interpretations by a great artist, but as the visual images suggested by Dante to a person much nearer the poet than we are, for the attitude of the Renaissance towards antiquity was still subjective—far less than Dante's, but endlessly more than our own. The Renaissance viewed antiquity not with our feeling of its being for ever past, but with longing and the hope of wholly restoring it to a living present. It is this which gives that fascinating tinge of romance to Renaissance reconstructions of antiquity. Michelangelo's attitude is already quite like our own, and his visual images could give no clue to Dante's; but as interpretations they would be invaluable, for he is the only artist of modern times whose genius was of a kind and of a quality to be compared with Dante's. That a series of illustrations by Michelangelo to the "Divina Commedia" existed there can be but little doubt, and their loss is one of the greatest the study of Dante has incurred. Botticelli's sketches are scarcely to be considered, for, great as they are as works of art, Botticelli was too subjective to give his illustrations a closer connection with the subject than can be had in lineal rhapsodies. Zuccaro and Stradano, working when the Renaissance was rotten-ripe, far from being a help, are as much in the way as Doré. They were even farther from suspecting the difference between their own and Dante's visual images. The next great event in the study of Dante will probably be an edition of the "Commedia" with illustrations chosen from the finest of the fourteenth and fifteenth centuries, and from the best by Signorelli and Botticelli, supplemented by such parallel conceptions as may be found in Dante's contemporaries, and even in Michelangelo and Tintoretto. The editor of such an edition of the "Commedia" will find that the ground has been well prepared by Dr. Ludwig Volkmann, in his pamphlet on early illustrations to Dante.[1]

Dr. Volkmann has examined more than seventy illustrated codices in Germany and Italy, not having extended his studies beyond these countries. France and England would have increased the list considerably. He divides the codices into two classes, those containing illuminations and such as have water-colour or lineal illustrations. The "Inferno," as might have been expected, attracted the greatest number of illustrators, the "Purgatorio" fewer, and the "Paradiso" least of all. Traditional compositions, therefore, as for ecclesiastical subjects, sprang up for the first, while the illustrator of the last had to rely on his own invention. But it seems to have taken a whole generation before illustrators found out what parts of the "Commedia" they could handle. At first they tried all the cantos.

Illuminated codices contain, as a rule, miniatures for the initial letters only at the beginning of each of the three sections, and these miniatures soon became stereotyped. In the initial of the "Inferno" Dante is represented either at his desk, or with Virgil in the forest. The P of the "Purgatorio" contains either Virgil and Dante sailing up to the Mount, or a picture of souls aflame. The L of the "Paradiso" gives a bust of Christ, the Trinity, or Dante and Beatrice. A few of the illuminated codices contain elaborate and very complete illustrations. Of the fourteenth century the best of all

---

[1] Bildliche Darstellungen zu Dantes Divina Commedia bis zum Ausgang der Renaissance." Leipzig; Breitkopf & Härtel, 1892. An extended and enlarged edition of this book appeared in 1897.

is one in the Nazionale at Florence, dating from about 1333. Here Minos, Pluto, and Cerberus are represented not as we who have been brought up on Smith's "Classical Dictionary" think of them, but as creatures with hoofs, claws and horns, and flaming eyes, as Dante in all probability saw them in his mind. A codex in the Angelica at Rome is almost on a level with the one in Florence. Among miniatured codices of later days the most valuable is certainly the one in the Vatican that was begun for Frederic of Urbino by some follower of Giovanni Bellini, and finished at a much later date by someone who was no stranger to Lorenzo Lotto's works. This codex would yield a number of plates for an illustrated edition of Dante.

The great difference between the illustrations in miniature and those in outline or water-colour is that the former never represent the same person more than once in the same illustration, while the latter tend to be *panoramic*, crowding several events in which the same person is concerned into one composition. (This, by the way, was a practice common to Italian painting in general.) The best of this latter series is a codex in the Marciana at Venice, with 245 large illustrations, for the most part in outline, by an artist who shows great affinities with the Florentines of the Trecento. At the beginning of the *Paradiso* he has represented Dante at the feet of Apollo, who appears here as a young, fair-haired knight fiddling to his heart's content. Most of the other illustrations are equally remote from our own conceptions and probably equally close to Dante's visual images.

The early engravings, such as Baldini's, have small value except as playthings, and the early woodcuts are scarcely better, although they often

have inimitable traits of naïveté ; but the conceptions of their authors are too infantile to touch
Dante at all.   The first edition of Dante with
woodcuts appeared at Brescia in 1487. Repetitions
and improvements of this were published at Venice
in 1491, 1493, and 1497. Not to these late illustrators, however, but to those of the fourteenth
century must we turn if we would attempt to discover
what images stood before Dante's mind while he was
writing those imperishable lines which wake in us
visions perhaps not less vivid, although so different
from his own.

SOME COMMENTS ON CORREGGIO
IN CONNECTION WITH HIS PICTURES IN
DRESDEN.[1]

A FEW years ago it would have been hard to tell which of the two, Correggio's "Night" or Raphael's "Madonna Di San Sisto," was the favourite picture of the Dresden Gallery. The little sanctuary where the Virgin with Saint Sixtus floats above the pseudo-altar was crowded with worshippers then, as it is now, while Correggio's picture had a no less large and devout following. But some change in popular taste has evidently taken place, for to-day few or none are found to linger before the "Night."

What inference is to be drawn? Was the enthusiasm for Correggio merely a fashion which has had its season? Why is it that he is no longer admired as he was in the first few decades of this century, in the day when no gentleman could afford to be without his theory of the "Correggiosity of Correggio?" In the explanation of the rise of his popularity may be found the answer to these questions.

The enthusiasm for Correggio dates from the time when, in Italian art, all the possible variations had been played upon the themes introduced by Raphael and Michelangelo, and the Caracci, in search for

[1] The Madonna with St. Francis, No. 150.
The Madonna with St. Sebastian, No. 151.
The Nativity, called the "Night," No. 152.
The Madonna with St. George, No. 153.

unhackneyed inspiration, betook themselves to a comparatively unlaboured field. They founded upon Correggio their school of painting, and thus succeeded in giving a further lease of life to Italian art. Correggio's interpreters, however, proved far more interesting to their contemporaries than the master himself, for average human beings have a strong tendency to appreciate only what is of their own day. The Caracci, Domenichino, Guercino, Guido Reni, and Lanfranco used up all the æsthetic capacity of their admirers, who believed in Correggio as the Catholic peasant doubtless believes in God, although he makes his offerings to the Saints. But in fairness it should be added that it was by no means easy to know the master himself. Correggio lived to be scarcely forty. Of his pictures then known the earliest dates from his twenty-first year, and in a career of barely twenty years no painter could have painted enough to fill the various collections of Europe. Nevertheless, a little later, towards the third decade of this century, the few whose word was law in matters of taste suddenly turned away from Guido, Lanfranco, and their like, and gave themselves up to an unbridled enthusiasm for the Caracci and for their master, Correggio; and later still, even the Caracci dropped out of sight, and Correggio stood alone.

This change was chiefly due to the fact that Correggio at last found in Toschi, the engraver, a perfectly accurate translator and publisher. If engraving be considered as a fine art by itself, there have been many greater masters of the craft than Toschi; but no one ever assimilated more thoroughly than he the style of a great painter of several centuries before, or ever gave such faithful, such impersonal renderings from an old master. When his engravings had made

it really possible to know Correggio, the public
placed him at once in the highest heaven. Nor, in
this instance, were they wrong. The Correggio with
whom they thus made acquaintance, the painter of
the frescoes in the Convent of St. Paul at Parma—
frescoes filled with delightful Cupids playing hide-
and-seek in garlands of flowers,—had a genius quite
as fine as any artist of his time.

Toschi's garlands and Cupids must have been
tantalizing to the lovers of Correggio, for the
originals were far away. Fortunately there were
several Correggios in Dresden, which was near at
hand, especially to the various seats of æsthetics,
such as Jena, Weimar, and Göttingen. In one of
the Dresden pictures both the Cupids and the garlands were to be seen, and this picture, the so-called
"St. George," became at once a favourite, and was,
of course, considered a masterpiece. But there is
still another reason, perhaps even more cogent, for
the sudden popularity of the "St. George." A
change in taste is no more completed in a day than
a change in character. The "St. George" is one of
Correggio's latest paintings, and, as followers always
take up a master's methods where he left them, this
picture was one of those upon which the Caracci
formed their own style. People were well acquainted with the Caracci : so they found it easy to
appreciate a work in which Correggio differs but little
from them. The "St. George" was painted about
1532, two years before Correggio's death. It represents the Madonna seated upon a throne of very
baroque design, surrounded by St. George and other
Saints. Her face is flabby and puffy, though not
without a certain charm, and her eyes are very large.
Her knees and her breast come close together : you
can almost see the soles of her feet. To understand

her appearance you must imagine yourself looking up at her from the bottom of a well.

When Correggio painted this picture he had already finished his frescoes in the dome of the Cathedral of Parma. These are so full of movement, contain such startling feats of foreshortening, that the painter of them seems to have fallen a victim to the admiration of his own cleverness. At any rate, he never afterwards drew a figure in repose, or in a normal position. He seemed to have used up his natural vein of feeling, and having used it up, his interest narrowed itself down to making his compositions animated and grandiose, debasing the human figure to purposes as vile as the contorted atlantides of baroque architecture. When this happens, when a painter is possessed by the desire to exhibit his cleverness, there is little further to be said about him as an artist.

But the picture had a further charm which appealed strongly to the connoisseurs of the day. To understand it, we need an idea of the dominant spirit of German literature during the twenties, when its principal exponents were Novalis, Fouqué, Tieck, and the Schlegels, Goethe's reign having passed, Heine's having not yet begun. It was the decade of pure Romanticism, and Romanticism, in Germany, was by no means that innocent, rough-and-tumble movement of liberation from prim manners and bad couplets that it was in England. The heroine of Miss Austen's " Northanger Abbey " is a much better representative of English romanticism than the somewhat hectic Marianne of " Sense and Sensibility." But even Marianne would have seemed a very coarse creature to the cultivators of the " Blue Flower." German romanticism carried sensibility to the point where it becomes insanity. Health was thought vulgar.   It was the fashion to seem diaphanous, to cough tellingly, to look worlds, and to take the greatest interest in what was of no human concern. The St. George in Correggio's picture was not diaphanous or consumptive, to be sure, but he certainly had the morphine habit, which would make him quite as interesting.   The children, with their huge heads and watery eyes, are monsters that might have been suggested by some fantastic tale of Hoffman's.   St. Peter Martyr talks theology with the sincerity of August von Schlegel, and St. John is sufficiently like Antinous preparing for a ballet to have rejoiced Wilhelm von Schlegel, the Göttingen professor of æsthetics.   The only figure in the picture that has any health in him is St. Gemigniano, and he hides in the background as if ashamed of being so robust.   For these literary reasons, then, the " St. George " became the standard, the canon of Correggio, and his other pictures were judged accordingly.   The " Night," being nearest to it, came next in public favour.   Indeed, when Romanticism began to go out of fashion, it became the supreme favourite, and rivalled in popularity even Raphael's Madonna.

This altar-piece was painted at least two years before the " St. George." The subject is the Nativity —a subject so often painted that Correggio might well have asked himself how he was to avoid the commonplace in treating it once more.   I am inclined to think that the painter tried to interpret the divine event from a point of view as human and lowly as that of the Gospels themselves.   The Madonna is in the first place a young mother, the Child is a mere human infant, and the Shepherds are nothing but shepherds.   St. Joseph, instead of being the usual supernumerary, is occupied in leading away a mule, who lingers, attracted by the light, or perhaps by the straw. There is no conventional choir of angels. His angels are too wild with joy to pose languidly with mandolins in their hands. It was the sheer humanity of this picture that drew so many pilgrims to it, and not, as the critics of that time said, because Correggio had the wonderful idea of making all the light stream from the Infant's face. Correggio may have had some such purpose, only as an intention it is rather literary than pictorial, and it is more likely that he had something in mind far less theological and poetical. His idea seems to have been to experiment with lights. From the Child's face the light streams out into the darkness, and dies away just before it encounters the first white of dawn appearing over the horizon. In the present condition of the picture, it is no longer possible to judge what was the effect. That it must have been very wonderful there can be no doubt. But even if the effect of the meeting of half lights and reflected lights at a point darker than either could still be appreciated, it would remain true that not the lights, but the human interpretation of the subject, maintained the popularity of the " Night." Art never changes, but the illustrative element of art may vary from generation to generation, and although a part of the explanation of this picture's fall from grace is doubtless due to the fact that a real feeling for artistic treatment as distinct from literature is much more widespread than it used to be, another conspiring cause has surely been that we nowadays demand of the literature of sacred scenes that it should be either more solemn or more naïve than in these examples of Correggio's art. But if the demand for a different literary interpretation of sacred legends and the growing appreciation of painting as painting makes it no longer possible for most people to be very enthusiastic about these two pictures, once so much admired, does it mean that there is nothing at all left to enjoy in Correggio? By no means!

As the knowledge of the old masters advances, and as, with the aid of discriminating criticism, the power to enjoy them increases, it is felt more and more that the latest works of a painter are not necessarily his best. Indeed it would seem that many of the Italian masters were most fascinating soon after they began to paint, or, at any rate, while they were still young. This was especially true of painters such as Correggio, who were more sensitive, perhaps, than vigorous—lyric rather than epic.

The Dresden gallery possesses a picture by Correggio which the leaders of æsthetics in the early decades of this century scarcely deigned to notice. It was done in 1514, in his twenty-first year, and being so early a work, it deserves our careful attention. It represents the Madonna with the Child in her lap, enthroned under an arch, with four Saints at her feet, St. Catherine and John the Baptist on her left, and St. Francis and St. Anthony of Padua to the right. Above, just under the arch, two little angels are poised in the air, as if it were water in which they floated joyfully at their ease. Between them is a halo, or glory, with ruddy cherubs peeping out from the straw-coloured light. The little angels are restful, the Child is quiet and simple, as different as possible from the nervous imp in the "St. George." The Madonna has a face in which there is nothing mystifying, nothing theatrical. The poses of the Saints are dramatic, their interest is very quick; but they are not at all so melo-dramatic as even Raphael's St. John in the "Madonna degli Ansidei," in the National Gallery. The scheme of

colour is bright and clear, but quiet. The arch
behind the throne opens upon an unobtrusive landscape. Although this is not among the severest
nor yet among the most majestic altar-pieces ever
painted, it is one of the most delicate and most felt.
Modern criticism takes this early work as a starting
point for the study of Correggio. A few years ago
it was supposed, indeed, to be his earliest painting;
but to-day we know nine or ten which he must have
done before. But as it was the study given to the
" St. Francis " which led to the discovery of the
earlier paintings, we can do nothing better than stop
here and see what this picture can reveal of Cor-
regio's history.

You cannot look long at the picture without the
haunting feeling of having seen elsewhere something
very much like it. The truth is that the St. Catherine here bears a strong resemblance to Raphael's
" St. Catherine " in the National Gallery, and the
St. John is not unlike the St. John in his " Madonna
di Foligno," of the Vatican. Other resemblances
might be traced; but these are enough.

The phenomena of art are as certainly governed
by laws as the phenomena of nature. One of the
tasks of art criticism is to discover these laws, which
prove that in art, as in nature, there is no such thing
as mere coincidence. Striking resemblances such
as these must be accounted for. It is of course out
of the question that Correggio was the pupil of
Raphael; but recent researches have given us the
clue to the real connection between them. It is
now admitted that Raphael owes much of what is
characteristic in his style to his first master, Timoteo
Viti, and, through him, to Francesco Francia and
Lorenzo Costa, Timoteo's teachers at Bologna. Correggio's training has been traced to the same sources,

for he also was, directly or indirectly, the pupil of
Costa and Francia.

On the wall opposite to the "St. Francis" hangs
a characteristic picture by Francia—"The Baptism
of Christ." The moment your attention is called to
it, you perceive that the movement of the figures in
both pictures is strikingly the same ; that the eyes
in both are opened wide in the same way, and that
the general scheme of colour is not unlike, the reds
and yellows, indeed, being identical. Correggio's
is finer, subtler, more delicate, but they differ only as
members of the same family.

The influence of Francia, however, does not explain everything in Correggio's picture. The Madonna's face, for instance, suggests Costa's type,
rather than Francia's, and the figure of Moses in
the medallion on the throne is taken almost direct
from Costa. The medallion itself, the elaborate
throne, the bas-reliefs on its base, are all of them
peculiar to Costa and to the Ferrarese school from
which he came ; and their presence in a picture by
Correggio is sufficient ground for placing him among
the painters of the school of Ferrara.

But Correggio used to be described as a Lombard
painter whose first master was a certain Bianchi,
but who owed his real training to Mantegna. Mantegna, however, died in 1506, when Correggio was
scarcely twelve years old. At that age, precocious
even as he was, he could scarcely have done more
than acquire the rudiments of his craft, and it is not
likely that instruction received so young would have
finally determined his style. Nor, indeed, is there
much in the "St. Francis" to indicate a personal
relation between Correggio and Mantegna. The
pose of the Madonna, it is true, is taken from
Mantegna's "Vierge Des Victoires" now in the

Louvre, which Correggio could have seen nowhere else than at Mantua. Poses, however, or even whole episodes, borrowed from another painter, no more prove direct descent than, for instance, the Latin words we have borrowed prove that English was derived from Latin.

But although there is no ground for the belief that Correggio was a pupil of Mantegna, the "St. Francis" confirms the old theory about Bianchi. The young painter was taught, just as children are taught writing, to draw the human form after a set fashion, especially such parts as the hands and ears, which are very obvious, and yet, when looked at carelessly, without much individuality. Naturally the method was the master's own, and the pupil kept it all his life, in spite of gradual and great variation. This fixed manner of drawing the hands and ears often assists us greatly in seeing the connection between a painter, his master, and his pupils, or in determining the authorship of a picture. You cannot look at the hands in the "St. Francis" without noticing not only that they are well modelled, that they are refined, but that the second finger of each is too long. Even if this were a personal idiosyncrasy, it is not an accident, for it is found in most of Correggio's pictures. Bianchi, whom the legend mentions as Correggio's teacher, is now being rediscovered after having been almost forgotten for centuries. His masterpiece, which shows that he was a painter of the Ferrarese school, is a "Madonna and Saints" in the Louvre. Few pictures even of that wonderful collection can surpass it for grandeur of composition, subtlety of feeling, clearness of colour, and quietness of tone. The flesh colour is very white. Make it less smooth, model it a little more, and you have the unrivalled flesh of the "Antiope"

Correggio's greatest achievement in flesh painting. The hands in this picture by Bianchi are not only shaped somewhat like the hands in the " St. Francis," but they have also the same characteristic, the elongated second figure. This goes a great way to prove that the legend was right in calling Bianchi Correggio's first master. Another thing that a pupil learned to do after a set fashion was the landscape. In the " St. Francis," the landscape is in tone and colour, if not altogether in drawing, identical with that in Bianchi's Madonna. Indeed, Correggio, allowing for the advances he made of himself in the differentiation of light, and in aerial perspective, remains always true to this type. In tone and colour the landscape even of the "St. George," painted, it will be remembered, two years before his death, is much like Bianchi's.

Correggio probably left Bianchi and went to Francia and Costa at Bologna in 1508, when he was fourteen years old. In 1509 Costa went to Mantua to take the place left vacant by Mantegna, and there is good reason to believe that Correggio went with him and remained there for several years. We have already seen that the " St. Francis " suggests his presence at Mantua before 1514, and a still earlier picture, belonging to Signor Crespi of Milan confirms the proof; for two of its figures—St. Elizabeth and the Infant John—are taken directly from Mantegna's picture which still hangs in his mortuary chapel at Mantua. Correggio's stay in Mantua brought him in contact with a painter under whose inspiration his work took on a character which was altogether more modern than Costa's. This painter was Dosso Dossi, who was in Mantua in 1511 and 1512. His influence can be traced in the whole series of Correggio's early pictures which

ends with the " St. Francis." In this altar-piece the
peculiar colour of the halo, like pale sulphur, and
the ruddy cherubs which frame it in, are strikingly
like the halo and the cherubs in a small "Coronation
of the Virgin " by Dosso, which is also in the Dresden Gallery. The little angels below the globe in
Dosso's picture are posed in a way which suggests
at once the pose of the Christ Child in the " St.
Francis," and in nearly all the early Correggios—in
the " Holy Family " of Hampton Court, in the
" Madonna " of the Municipal Museum of Milan, in
the "Madonna and Saints" belonging to Signor
Frizzoni, also in Milan, in the " Madonna " at Pavia,
and in the " Madonna with Angels " of the Uffizi.

It would not be hard to weave a romance about
Correggio's relation to Dosso. In 1511 Dosso Dossi
was thirty-two years old, and nearly at the height of
his genius. It was just before he became the court
painter of Alfonzo of Ferrara and Lucretia Borgia,
his wife. Ariosto speaks of him in his "Orlando "
along with Giorgione and Leonardo and Michelangelo. The court poet and the court painter were
remarkably alike in the essence of their genius.
They were both lovers of " high romance," and
both had the power to create it—the one in verse,
the other in colour—with a splendour that perhaps
many other Italians could have equalled, but with a
fantasy, a touch of magic, that was more characteristic of English genius in the Elizabethan period
than of Italian genius at any time. Real feeling for
the fantastic and magical has not often been granted
to the well-balanced Italian mind. It is all the more
delightful, therefore, to find an artist who has not
only the strength and self-possession of an Italian,
but the romance and sense of mystery of the great
English poets. If Marlowe had written about Circe,

he would have presented us with one like Dosso's,
as she may be seen in the Borghese gallery: an
enchantress clothed in crimson and emerald, sitting
under balsamic trees where olive green lights are
playing, with the monsters about her feet, their real
natures made visible by her arts.   Rather than Greek
she is Arabian.   She does not permit us to ask
whether the lines of her form are classical, or whether
her form is statuesque.   Before her we lose ourselves
in a maze of strange lights and mysterious colours
which make us sink deeper and deeper into a world
which is as entrancing as it is far away.   Marlowe
and Shakespeare would have taken that delight in
her which we can well imagine Ariosto took.

   The painter of pictures like this could not help
having an extraordinary fascination over such a
sensitive, dreamy, ecstatic temperament as Correggio's.   It is easy to imagine the precocious lad of
sixteen, with his training already far advanced, but
with faculties interpretive rather than creative, falling
down in worship before the dazzling achievements
of the Ferrarese painter.   Dosso's personal charm,
also, must have been great, and he was just at the
point in his life when the man is the boy's ideal.
Fellow artists, then as now, we may be sure, talked
of nothing so much as of their craft.   Dosso, who
had been in contact with the Venetians, and with
pupils of Raphael, and was in touch with many of
the problems that interested the painters of the day
must undoubtedly have inspired Correggio with his
own interests.   Nothing occupied the best painters just
then so much as the problem of light—one of the eter-
nal problems of painting.   In Florence, Pier dei Franceschi, Verrocchio, and Leonardo ; and in Venice,
Alvise Vivarini, Carpaccio and Giorgione had brought
the treatment of light to a point far beyond any-

thing Correggio's teacher Costa could have known, and Dosso himself was behind none of them in daring experiments with light and atmosphere. It was just this advanced treatment which was necessary to give Correggio the means to develop his peculiar talent; for he was not destined to create new types or new subjects. It was his destiny rather to be among the first to treat his subject for the personal feeling and not for the mere action—still less for the mere composition. When he is at his best, he not only makes the face but the whole figure, and the landscape as well, the vehicle of emotion, and this to such a degree that to go beyond is to become a Guido Reni. But he never could have accomplished this with the limited acquaintance with light his first masters gave him. From Dosso he got the impulse for that study of the effects of light, which itself became in his hands a means of expression utterly undreamt of heretofore.

It is easy to trace this connection between them. In almost every picture of Dosso's, where the subject and composition permit (as, for instance, in the small "Coronation" already mentioned), the groups are so arranged that in looking at the landscape, one seems to be looking out upon it from within a cavern. This is the case to an even greater degree in a larger "Coronation" by Dosso, which hangs opposite to the "St. Francis." Where this cavern-like effect is not possible, Dosso used to light one part of his picture much more than the rest, as one may see in his "St. George," which hangs above the "St. Francis." In short, his pictures never present the appearance of the greater part of the paintings done before his day,—the appearance of an infinitesimally low relief. On the contrary, he batters great holes into his compositions, huge pockets, as it were, and fills them with light. To make the contrast even greater, he gives a slate-gray colour to the rim of this well of light, if not to the whole darker portion of the picture. Correggio took this treatment from Dosso, refined and advanced upon it, but Dosso's treatment of light and shadow contains in embryo all Correggio's.

The first instance of this in Correggio occurs in a picture already mentioned, belonging to Signor Crespi of Milan. It is a " Nativity." The Holy Child is lying in a wicker basket on the ground. The Virgin kneels beside Him. Two little angels are floating above, like the angels in the " St. Francis." To the left, from the direction where the light is breaking, two other angels lead up the pious shepherds. Not only does the light in this picture all stream from one corner, but the general tone is slate-gray. Looked at merely as light and tone it is identical with Dosso's " St. George." It is easy to see the same influence in many other details, as, for instance, in the drawing of the eyes and mouths, which Dosso, in his works, was inclined to make like black holes. This peculiar way of making the eyes and mouths, transmitted to Correggio, is even more clearly visible in a picture belonging to Mr. Robert Benson of London. It must have been painted somewhat later than the " Nativity." The subject is " Christ taking leave of His Mother." Clothed in white, He kneels with crossed arms at His mother's feet. She seems to be on the point of rushing forward to embrace Him, but is held back by Mary. The Virgin's face expresses the greatest grief, but nothing wild or unseemly. St. John stands a trifle back, with his hands clasped in sympathizing sorrow. The distribution of light here is even more Dossesque than

THE NATIVITY

in the " Nativity." It all comes from the left-hand
corner, whence it breaks over the Lake of Galilee,
broods upon its surface with a pale gray light, flashes
up to the sky in a greenish streamer, and is reflected
on Christ's raiment, and on His mother's face.

So we might take up Correggio's earliest paintings one after another, and find Dosso in them all.
I must mention one more at all events. It is an
" Epiphany" from the Archbishop's Palace in Milan,
now transferred to the Brera. At first glance, it is
hardly to be distinguished from a Dosso; but a
more careful examination leaves little doubt that it
is by the younger painter, who, in this instance,
seems to have caught, along with Dosso's way of
painting, something also of his feeling for the
romantic. Dosso's influence comes out again in
the " Rest in the Flight," painted a little before the
" St. Francis." Of the three pictures by Correggio
that the Uffizi possesses, this is by far the most
beautiful. The deep-set eyes, the pale sulphur
colour in the Madonna's robe, the dark wood, are
all reminders of Dosso, and the Virgin herself might
be half-sister to the " Circe."

Having deducted the story of Correggio's growth
bit by bit, from the survey of his pictures it will
perhaps not be found amiss to sum it up briefly.
Correggio got his rudiments from Bianchi, who
handed him on to Francia and Costa. Costa took
him to Mantua, where the works of Mantegna seem
to have made only a passing impression on him.
There he came in close contact with Dosso Dossi
who helped him to acquire a method of painting
which gave full scope to his genius. To complete
the account of the influences which went to form him,
it remains for me to speak of a picture in Munich—
the little " Faun "—so strikingly Venetian in char-

acter that Dosso's influence alone will not explain it. In colour it is like a Palma, in movement it is like a Lotto. It leads inevitably to the inference that Correggio must have visited Venice before finally settling down near Parma—an inference that might explain the puzzling likenesses between Lotto and Correggio that keep forcing themselves upon our attention.

Art is a flower of the human personality. Flower-like, it breathes out perhaps not its strongest, but often its most delicate, perfume soon after bursting. It is delicious to catch an artist's naïve impressions of the world, and this is one of the rewards of studying the earliest works of a painter. In the Italian Renaissance, at least, if a man was born with something to say in form and colour, he was likely to say the best of it very soon after he had fair mastery of his brush, rather than later, when manifold commissions, family concerns, and the ever-advancing invasion of the commonplace, made him think of his painting less as an art and more as a business.

This is above all the case with Correggio, whose genius was so distinctively subjective and lyrical. The pictures already discussed bring out this point clearly. The briefest comparison, for instance, between Signor Crespi's "Nativity," painted when Correggio was sixteen or seventeen, and the same subject as treated in the "Night," when he was thirty-five, shows that although he had made immense technical advances in the later picture, he had lost that intense and poetical religious feeling which made the early picture so impressive. Or, again, the "Rest in the Flight" of the Uffizi has a personal quality which somehow the later picture of the same subject at Parma, beautiful as it is, utterly lacks. In the first, you feel that Correggio tried to

CORREGGIO

CHRIST TAKING LEAVE OF HIS MOTHER

live the scene before painting it; in the other, that he is reciting it like a lesson well learned. Even in the " St. Francis " he had lost something of the religious imagination he had when he was at work on the picture of "Christ taking leave of His Mother." There he had an intensity of feeling and a reserve of expression which we no longer find in the later picture, where the feeling is much more ordinary and the expression at the same time a little exaggerated.

Another advantage of studying a painter from his beginnings arises from the fact that there is a large intellectual element even in pleasure supposed to be purely æsthetic. A painter naturally shows more clearly at first than afterwards how he is connected with the other painters of his time. We get to know his first forms, to see how they have come down to him from his teachers, and, finally, how they are transmitted by him to his pupils. If we learn to like his characteristics for their beauty and for their historical associations, we continue to like them, no matter how disguised. The ability to trace them in a picture makes that picture to some degree delightful in spite of the faults it may otherwise have. It is, for example, satisfactory to find in the "St. George" that the landscape and the hands still retain something of their early likeness to Bianchi. Although there is little left to enjoy in the "Night," yet an acquaintance with Signor Crespi's "Nativity" makes it most interesting to see how the painter treated the subject after a lapse of twenty years. So that the study of the early works of a master not only reveals him at a period when he is likely to be very charming, but makes him interesting even in his decadence.

It has not been my purpose to speak of the works

of Correggio's maturity. In the period between the "St. Francis" and the "St. George," he painted such pictures as the "Antiope" and the "Leda," the "Danaë," the "Io," and the "Ganymede," pictures as intensely lyric as his earliest are sincerely religious. It only remains to mention another picture in the Dresden Gallery dating from this same period. It is the so-called "St. Sebastian"—the Madonna on a throne with cherubs and angels about her, looking down upon St. Sebastian and two other saints. It is a picture with the same movement and the same feeling that we find in the "Leda," the "Io," or the "Danaë," even the face of the Madonna being very much like what the "Leda" must have been. Like all these masterpieces, it is full of that high-strung sensuous emotion which inevitably suggests the music of violins. But of course such movement and such feeling are utterly out of harmony with the subject of a religious picture, where the effect to be produced is one of awe and devotion, not of fellowship with the gods in ecstatic enjoyment.

CORREGGIO

[*Brera, Milan.*

THE ADORATION OF THE MAGI

THE FOURTH CENTENARY OF CORREGGIO[1]

FOUR centuries have elapsed since the birth of Correggio. Parma is celebrating the event by industrial exhibitions and agricultural shows. We may make a more appropriate use of the occasion by considering Correggio's real place in art—a task especially worth undertaking since he has evoked from diverse critics, on the one hand passionate praise, and on the other no less passionate blame.

Criticism may, however, occupy itself with other tasks than praise or blame. It should, for instance, endeavour to discover and define the artist's real capacities and qualities. Then, if our interest be merely personal, we can abandon ourselves to liking or disliking ; while if it be historical, we shall know what to think of the age which adored or abhorred the artist in question.

What, then, was the quality of Correggio's genius as revealed in his works ? To appreciate this quality we must first note with what other artists Correggio shared the Italian field of painting, and what influences went to form him.

At the beginning of the sixteenth century, Italy saw the rise, in every school, of painters in whose work the element of beauty and of real life so far outweighed the elements which were merely characteristic of their own school and epoch that their pictures,

[1] 1894.

even now, can be enjoyed with no special preparation. To appreciate Raphael, or Michelangelo, or Titian requires none of the education in history and in the art that one must have to appreciate such masters of the fifteenth century as the Vivarini, Pier dei Franceschi, or Botticelli. Correggio is one of the "modern" artists, and holds among the painters of the district between Bologna, Ferrara, and Parma the place that Raphael holds among the painters of central Italy, Michelangelo and Andrea del Sarto among the Florentines, or Titian and Lotto among the Venetians ; and he is as much the outcome of the artistic endeavour of that part of Italy as Andrea, Raphael, and Titian are of Tuscany, Umbria, and Venice.

Correggio may have got his rudiments from some local master in his native town, or in the neighbouring town of Modena; but in his very earliest paintings he shows himself as the unmistakable pupil of Costa and Francia, in whose workshop at Bologna he must already have been before 1509. In that year Costa went to Mantua, and probably took Correggio with him, for several pictures painted by Correggio in the next few years bear witness to the study of certain works by Mantegna which he could have seen in Mantua alone. At Mantua also he came in contact with a painter who saved him, perhaps, from becoming merely a perfected Costa or Francia. This was Dosso Dossi, an artist of great imaginative power, with a mastery of colour as splendid as that of any Venetian, and with a skill in the treatment of light and shadow at first almost unrivalled. He communicated an ardour to the young Correggio—whose own nature was from the first sensitive and lyrical—which prevented him from painting all the rest of his life pictures merely dreamy, sweet, and antiquated, such as Costa's. It was to Dosso, too, that Correggio owed the first impulse to that study of effects of light and shadow, and of aerial perspective, in which he afterwards went beyond everything that had been done before him.

The nine or ten pictures which Correggio painted before his twenty-first year show with remarkable clearness just what was his own personal quality and what he owed to his masters and to Dosso. The forms and types, nearly all that has to do with the mere design, come from Costa and Francia, while the treatment of light and shadow, and much of the colouring, is distinctly Dossesque. But the intensely felt religious emotion, impregnated with poetry, which is expressed in the faces and in the landscape accompaniments, is his own, and is as perfectly distinct from the dreaminess of Costa as from the fiery fancy of Dosso. These earliest works are his most genuinely religious pictures, and in all art it would be hard to find their equals for delicacy and sincerity of feeling. Their aim is not, like that of the religious paintings of earlier generations, to inspire us with contrition and awe, but to put us in sympathy with the marvellous poetry and the deep humanity of the story of Christ. All through his life Correggio's nature continued unchanged ; it remained sensitive and lyrical. When he had a subject to paint, he chose to dwell entirely upon the elements of feeling in it, and to express them with the utmost rapture. This may be called the law of his being, and he is completely satisfactory when the subject gives full scope for his genius, and less satisfactory when the subject does not lend itself to a rapturously emotional treatment.

In his youth, his lack of skill, his tentativeness, his immaturity, hampered him. He had not yet that mastery which afterwards enabled him at the same time to express all the rapture of feeling within him and to make it seem real. This required an extraordinary skill in draughtsmanship, and, above all, an understanding of light and shadow, which he attained only later, although early enough in his brief life. At first it was as if his only instrument had been the harp and he expressed only what the harp could express. But his means of expression increased until at last he had in his hands an instrument as powerful and as responsive as the orchestra. So in his early pictures, his expression of emotion was restrained and quiet, and was admirably suited to the religious subjects which he then treated. But in such a picture as the " Madonna with St. Francis " at Dresden, painted in his twenty-first year, the emotion is already a trifle too much for the subject. He represents the Madonna and saints, wishing to keep to the architectonic form of the conventional altar-piece. But the figures have so much feeling of their own to utter that they stand uneasily within the bounds of the prescribed composition. In such a picture, however, as the " Zingarella " at Naples, painted only a little later, where he had nothing to depict but the emotion of a mother passionately caressing her child, no touch of exaggeration is felt. So also with the " Nativity " in the Uffizi, painted a few years later, where there is nothing but a young mother trying to attract the attention of her little baby. Correggio is in fact faultless as an artist whenever the emotion he had to portray was purely human and joyous, no matter how refined or how ecstatic.

He spent the twelve most productive years of his life, from 1518 to 1530, at Parma, and there he found ample opportunity for the kind of painting in which he could give full swing to his genius for the expression of intense feeling. In the choir of San Giovanni he painted the Coronation of the Virgin. The Madonna here does not, as in the usual treat-

CORREGGIO

THE MADONNA OF ST. FRANCIS

ment of the subject, kneel like a meek handmaiden, crushed with the honour that is being conferred upon her, but throws herself into it with rapture, as into a joy of which she means to possess herself to the utmost. The St. John in the same church seems likewise to abandon himself to the ecstasy of his inspiration. In the cupola of the cathedral he painted his famous Ascension of the Virgin. She is surrounded by figures all striving to be on a level with her own intense exultation as she gives herself up to the unspeakable bliss of rising to the highest heaven. The abandonment to the utmost possible human joy is far greater here than even in Titian's "Assunta." Every one of the whole host of accompanying angels seems an embodiment of the jubilant triumph which the Virgin herself feels, and which sweeps through the whole universe at the same moment.

Having such a preference for a rapturously emotional treatment, Correggio was at his best only in such subjects as these, and not in subjects which required the expression of sorrow or of resignation. So, in a picture like the " Martyrdom of Placidus and Flavia " (in the Parma Gallery), Flavia abandons herself in an ecstatic vision, and is therefore one of the finest figures Correggio ever painted, while Placidus, who tries to look believing and resigned, succeeds only in looking jesuitical. In his one Pietà, also, Correggio is far from being at his best, although the dead Christ is a splendid figure, just because in him there is nothing that suggests sorrow or pain. Again, with such a preference for an emotional treatment, he naturally ended by choosing subjects in which there was nothing to fetter his full expression. These he found in the love stories of the gods ; and in his " Danaë," in his

" Io," and in his " Leda," he portrays human beings so utterly given up to an all-possessing emotion that they tremble with it as water trembles under a breeze.

It was his passion, too, for the expression of joyful feeling that led Correggio to seize every chance to paint *putti*—little children as artless and simple as real childhood, but bearing far greater joys than childhood ever felt.   His first commission at Parma was to decorate the parlour of the Convent of San Paolo ; and this he filled with *putti* peeping from behind trellises, sporting with garlands, and playing with instruments of the chase, all in eager sympathy with the huntress Diana, who forms the centre of the composition.   His success in this, no doubt, gained him the commissions that kept him so long in Parma ; for, from its beginnings, the Renaissance had made the *putto* the symbol of its own joy in life and of its own emotions, and a painter who put into his *putti* all the life, simplicity, and restlessness of real childhood, and at the same time all the immense rapture and joy in mere existence that Italy was feeling in the beginning of the sixteenth century, could not fail to be appreciated.

This intense and rapturous emotion might have become cloying in the end if Correggio had not always been as unstudied and as unconscious as he was emotional.   In his mere craftsmanship, too, he seems to have been the most unconscious of artists, never dreaming that he would be admired or blamed for his astonishing foreshortenings, or for his broad, almost modern, treatment of light and shadow.   In this, indeed, he had scarcely a rival, even among the later Venetians. None of them, not even Tintoretto, treated effects of diffused light with such success as he.   In his ripe years he loved effects of broad day-

light and landscapes sparkling with sunshine, as if
he could not have light enough to bring Nature into
complete harmony with his own rapture. His landscapes seem therefore to pulsate with joy under the
full sunlight, and he gives fields and trees that look
of gaiety which they have in the early summer.

His colouring was throughout on a level with the
intense joyfulness of his feeling and with his sunny
landscapes. Distinct from the Venetians, he was in
no way inferior to them, except that colour and
brushwork did not with him, as it did with the
Venetians, become a distinct instrument of expression. But where he is unrivalled, either by them
or perhaps by any other Italian painters, is in the
flesh painting of the one or two perfectly preserved
pictures which we still have. Flesh that looks so
real as that of the " Antiope " in the Louvre, it would,
perhaps, be hard to find anywhere else.

Correggio's genius, as we have seen, was throughout emotional and lyrical. Lyrical feeling rarely goes
with the power of unemotional observation such as
good portraiture requires. It is not surprising, therefore, that not a single portrait by Correggio exists.

It happens that the English poets afford striking
parallels to the Italian painters. Thus, there is a
decided similarity of genius between Shakespeare
and Titian, and between Michelangelo and Milton.
A lover of these poets cannot help finding the cor-
responding painters much more intelligible. But
centuries had to elapse before emotions so intense
as those Correggio felt found expression in literature—in Shelley when he is at his best, and in Keats
when he is perfect.

AMICO DI SANDRO

THERE exists a group of Florentine pictures dating
from the seventh and the following decade of the
fifteenth century, which at present pass under the
names of Filippo Lippi, Botticelli, Ghirlandajo and
Filippino Lippi. The pictures of this whole group
are, nevertheless, in spite of their diverse naming,
intimately connected one with another. Let us
examine the more important of these works with the
object of seeing whether they may not be by the
same painter, and, if they are, what they can reveal
regarding his artistic personality.

The earliest of these pictures is at Naples (Sala
Toscana, No. 32), a Madonna with two angels holding
the Child. The composition and the idea were no
doubt suggested by the beautiful " Madonna with
Angels " (in the Uffizi), of the painter to whom, until
recently, this Naples panel also was attributed,
namely, Fra Filippo. But Filippo's winsome gaiety
has here given place to a heavy melancholy, a
dolorous yearning, which exaggerate the mood at
times expressed by Botticelli. To the latter the
Naples Madonna is now ascribed, and not without
a show of reason. The types and the landscape
recall such early works of Sandro's as Prince Chigi's
" Madonna" and the Berlin " St. Sebastian." The
drawing of the pupil of the eye and shape of the
ear remind us of Botticelli's even earlier " For-
tezza," and the angel's drapery has considerable

[*Naples Museum.*

VIRGIN AND CHILD WITH TWO ANGELS

THE CHIGI MADONNA

resemblance to the drapery in his two little pictures
with the story of " Judith." Nevertheless the attribution of the Naples panel to Sandro himself is an
error. It is inferior in quality to even his most
tentative paintings, and, looked at closer, it betrays
the imitator rather than the inventor of a style.
The outlines here are uneven, either needlessly hard,
or not sufficiently firm. The artist finds peculiar
difficulty in drawing the nose, and has not here succeeded in rendering a single one which does not
attract attention to itself through some fault. The
hair is arranged like a wig, and lacks the plasticity
which Botticelli seldom failed to give it. Very
niggling and unworthy of any great master is the
edge of the draperies, as, for instance, in the Virgin's
hood.[1] The modelling of the exposed parts is timid,
and of the rest of the figures wretched. There is
scarcely a suggestion of bodies under the clothing.[2]
Then the colour is quite unlike Sandro's. The
flesh is ruddy brown, the hair almost auburn, the
landscape bronzed, and the draperies either a very
pale mauve, or a red as bright as Ghirlandajo's.
This picture, in short, reveals the existence of a
painter who towards 1475 was imitating Botticelli
closely, a painter not at all contemptible, but dependent, and of uneven attainment. Thus far his
peculiar individuality is manifested in little more
than in his colouring. We shall meet with his ruddy
browns and pale mauves again and again. In all

[1] This we find again in a later work by the same hand, "The
Five Virtues," in the Corsini Gallery (No. 340), ascribed to
Botticelli. (Photo. Alinari.)
[2] How different is Sandro in all these points will be readily
perceived by any competent person who will take the trouble to
compare this picture with a Madonna that Botticelli himself
painted at about this time—I refer to the one which until recently
belonged to Prince Chigi.

else he merely debases Sandro's forms and surcharges his sentiment.[1]

"The Madonna with the youthful Baptist and two Angels" in the collection from Santa Maria Nuova, now in the Uffizi (Photo. Alinari), attributed to Fra Filippo, and given by recent writers to Botticelli, need not detain us, for, although it certainly is by the hand that painted the Naples picture, and is furthermore of the same time, it has been so thoroughly renovated that of the original surface there is little to be perceived. That little, however, points to an even blonder tone, such as we shall find presently in the Turin "Three Archangels." We can occupy ourselves meanwhile with the most interesting and best preserved of our Anonimo's early Madonnas, the one ascribed to Ghirlandaio, belonging to Mrs. Austen (Capel Manor, Horsmonden, Kent). The Virgin, here again heavily brooding, sits sideways on a parapet against an arched porch opening out on a river valley. The Child stands on her lap and embraces her. An angel, all wonder and yearning, looks on. The Virgin and the Child are not very different from the same figures in the Naples picture, yet even as types they show a considerable advance. The Madonna has the same heavy eyelids; the Child's arm is drawn exactly in the same faulty way as in the Naples and Santa

---

[1] An amusing point in proof that we have to do here with an imitator, is the elaborate architectonic seat. It will be noticed that not only is the perspective curious, but that at the corner there goes up a sort of partition which leads nowhere. True, the halo, conceived as untransparent, would hide the structure in part, but it should reappear above, or, if supposed to stop first, the continuation of whatever it supports should appear to the right. The painter has forgotten to do either, in his listless imitation of a motive which, without understanding it, he took from such an one of Botticelli's early pictures as Prince Chigi's.

MADONNA AND CHILD WITH ST. JOHN

Maria Nuova panels; but the modelling is less hard, and the outlines begin to be a little blurred and somewhat sketchy. Note also the steep shoulder of the Madonna. The folds are simpler, indicating that the painter, closely following Botticelli, his model, was beginning to turn back from Pollajuolo and Verrocchio to the traditions of Fra Filippo. Indeed the golden flesh, the golden brown hair, and the mauve of the Child's tunic produce an effect of light tone never paralleled in Botticelli, which would seem to point to a person who had got a strong bias for this scheme of colour under Filippo, while the latter was painting such a work as his " Dance of Salome" at Prato. There remains, by the way, a curious detail of resemblance between our painter and Filippo Lippi. Everyone will have remarked the absurd perspective of the vase in Filippo's " Annunciation " now at the National Gallery. The vase in Mrs. Austen's picture certainly is not so bad, yet it clearly is derived from that.

From an almost characterless imitator of Botticelli, our Anonimo becomes, in the next of his pictures that we encounter, a distinct artistic personality. He still reminds us of Sandro, but only in a slight degree more than of Pollajuolo and Verrocchio. He reveals a gayer, more easy-going temperament than Sandro's. He does not take his art at all so earnestly, is something of an improviser, holds indeed a similar position to Botticelli and as distinct from his as, in two or three generations later, Rosso will have to Andrea del Sarto. The picture which reveals all this is the " Three Archangels "[1] in the Turin Gallery, ascribed to Botti-

---

[1] A drawing for this picture, ascribed to Pollaiuolo, is exhibited in the His de la Salle Collection in the Louvre. This is by no means the only sketch by our Anonimo in existence, but I shall

celli. The composition is not taken from, but may have been suggested by the famous Verrocchiesque picture in the Florence Academy, which, after having passed for centuries as Botticelli's, is now being fast accepted as Botticini's. But the Turin panel has none of the mincing uncouthness of that work ; the figures are slim and graceful; the faces are more expressive, and indeed the Archangel Raphael's solicitude could scarcely be depicted better; the head of Tobias is most lovely. The colouring is gay and fresh, with mauve and gold predominating. The movement of the group is full of spring. The points of contact with our Anonimo's earlier works are not few. The greatest similarity will be found in the heads, with their square jaws, pointed chins, faulty noses, their not faultlessly drawn mouths, and, most of all, the hair curling and yet as of a wig. The draperies also bear witness to the identity of authorship. Compare, for instance, the folds in Michael's mantle with the folds in Mrs. Austen's picture. Between this last work, moreover, and " The Archangels " there is a connection not only as I already have said in tone, but in the landscape as well.[1]

In this Turin picture the painter dashes, in a fashion, ahead of Botticelli. Executed in all probability before 1480, there are not lacking here touches which in Sandro are found only at the end of his career. The draped legs, for instance, of Gabriel and Raphael are more like those of the dancing angels in Sandro's " Nativity " of 1500 (National

speak of them all in detail in my forthcoming book on Florentine Drawings.

[1] Signor Cavalcaselle is too characteristic about this picture not to be quoted : " It recalls the manner of Botticelli's pupils, perhaps that of Filippino Lippi, *or of some other pupil of said Filippino Lippi.*" (" Storia della Pittura," vi. 282.)

Turin Gallery.

TOBIAS AND THE ARCHANGELS

AMICO DI SANDRO

Louvre, Paris.

STUDY FOR A TOBIAS WITH THE ARCHANGELS

Gallery) than of any of his earlier figures. The
sweep of Tobias' mantle also would, in Botticelli,
point to a later date. We are thus led to suspect
that our Anonimo was a sort of feebler Sandro,
describing a smaller orbit about a kindred artistic
purpose, and therefore travelling with greater speed
through its signs. He would suggest a person of
rapid development, and what so often occasions it, a
life destined to be brief, and as if aware that it has
but a little span wherein to accomplish its desires.

The same suggestion of a sudden maturity, but
with a curious harking back to first impressions, is
conveyed by a lunette with a picture of the "Coronation," belonging to the Marquess of Lothian (New
Gallery Portfolio, 1894, No. 80). The God the
Father here, not only in type, but in his draperies,
recalls Fra Filippo. The Madonna, on the other
hand, suggests Botticelli's "Coronation," and the
angels who hold the curtain aside bring to mind the
same master's "Madonna with St. Catherine and
other Saints" of the Florence Academy, and the
"Nativity" of the Ambrosiana, all of them probably of
a later date than Lord Lothian's lunette. On the other
hand, there is much here which suggests a close following upon Sandro's early *tondo* of the "Adoration"
in the National Gallery (No. 1033), as, for instance,
the folds with large loops. The heads and busts
of the angels are almost copies of the figure in the
same *tondo* of the youth seen full length, on the left,
holding by the bit the large horse. Lord Lothian's
picture is ascribed to Fra Filippo, but in colour, in
style (such as it has), and in quality it is so like the
Turin "Archangels" that other writers have already
noted the identity of hand.[1] It is, however, a some-

---

[1] Dr. Ulmann in Repert. Kunstw. xvii., p. 490. Signor
Cavalcaselle says of it that its "execution is inferior, and its colour

what more advanced work, and nearer to Botticelli.

A similar mingling of elements that in Botticelli
would belong both to the beginning and to the end
of his career, meets us in two *cassone* panels which
must have been painted by our Anonimo at about
this time (toward or just after 1480). One is in the
Pitti and represents the "Death of Lucretia" (Photo.
Alinari, 2916); the other, in the Louvre, contains the
"Story of Virginia" (Photo. Braun, 1684). In both
the action is almost as vehement, and the movement
as rapid as in the two larger panels treating the same
subjects which Botticelli was to paint a number of
years later. Yet, examined closely, our Anonimo's
pictures reveal decided affinities with Sandro's "Adorations," all of them relatively early works. The
groups to right and to left of the Decemvir in one panel,
of Lucretia in the other, have close resemblances to the
groups of worthy burgesses in Sandro's two " Adorations " at the National Gallery (Nos. 592 and 1033,
the latter ascribed to Filippino). The folds of the
draperies in the *cassoni* are Filippesque, as in these
" Adorations." Of course the same folds have even
greater resemblance to those in Lord Lothian's "Coronation," or in the " Three Archangels." Both the
Virginia and the Lucretia stories are ascribed to
Filippino. Signor Cavalcaselle, whose power of observation so frequently surpassed his faculty for
drawing the proper conclusions, remarks that these
paintings " recall the manner of Fra Filippo, and
might be by Filippino" ("Storia" vii., p. 98). But they
recall Filippo far too much to be by Filippino. They
are by a painter on whom Filippo must have made a

lacks vigour, wherefore we believe that it was painted for the
master by some assistant of his, perhaps Fra Diamante." ("Storia,"
v., p. 241.)

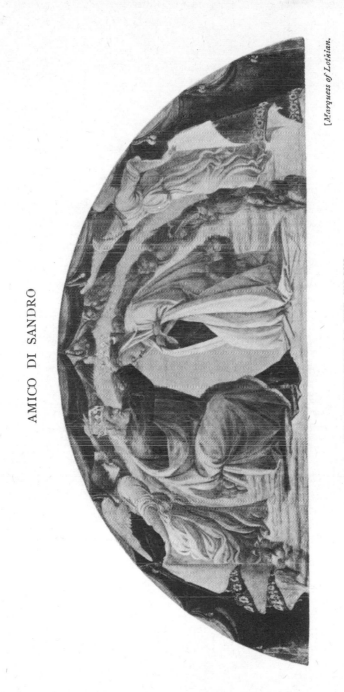

AMICO DI SANDRO

THE CORONATION OF THE VIRGIN

far more lasting impression than he had time to make on his own son.

Before going further, I shall point out the clear connections between these two pictures and our Anonimo's earlier works. Nearest to them stand the " Archangels " and the " Coronation." The Tobias you will be able, so to speak, to multiply again and again into the two *cassone* fronts. The folds of Michael's cloak are as near as may be to those in the Decemvir's mantle. The stride of the other two angels, with their legs clearly indicated under the draperies, you will find matched again and again in the " Story of Virginia." The colour is of that golden brown tone for which our Anonimo has shown a continuous preference. The elaborate, but simply drawn, architecture we also have met with before, in Mrs. Austen's " Madonna," for instance. Thus, while these panels have more than enough in common with the pictures which we already have discussed to establish that they are all by the same hand, they yet reveal, and for the first time, certain peculiarities which we shall find constantly recurring in the later works. These *cassone* panels are more sketchy than the earlier pictures, and produce, as do so many of our painter's later performances, an effect almost of being blurred The landscape, which, by the way, is strictly consequent upon such an one as in Mrs. Austen's " Madonna," is not only somewhat blurred but is spotted as well. Then we note a decided preference for elaborate architectonic backgrounds, and a curious fondness for openings, not only such as doors and windows, but in pillars, and these our Anonimo loved to paint, as if seen in very steep perspective, and, when possible, with light streaming through them. But the most singular and most characteristic of all the peculiarities here visible are the tall, so to speak, rectangular heads, and the faces with their beetling brows, deepset eyes, pointed noses, and general look of vehemence. Some one or more of these traits we shall meet with in all the pictures which we shall now examine.

Almost contemporary in date with the last two, is the "Adoration" in the National Gallery (No. 1124) which at Hamilton Palace was attributed to Botticelli —an attribution somewhat nearer the mark, on the whole, than the one to Filippino which it now bears. It is a quaint, fresh, and charming work. The scene takes place in the nearest foreground of a rocky landscape somewhat blurred and vague in outline, and of pale colour. It is alive with passers by, and fixed anchorites. Although in ruins, the shed is drawn with our author's fondness for linear perspective. With the exception of one old man who is exactly like the God the Father in Lord Lothian's "Coronation," and of a young king kneeling on the left who resembles the angels in the same picture, all the figures are of the peculiar type I have just described. The horses are perfectly identical with those in the "Story of Virginia." The Madonna, however, is the first figure that we have yet encountered in this group of pictures, which distinctly suggests Filippino. Of this, more later. For the present, note that small wriggling folds begin to take parasitical possession of the draperies, as in the draperies of the kneeling kings.[1]

A still further advance, a tone more richly golden, folds more petty and wriggling, drawing more sketchy and blurred, is shown in a series of panels with the

---

[1] I am acquainted with several copies of this picture painted in the second quarter of the sixteenth century, the best of them being in the Sterbini collection at Rome, done by some artist who suggests both Bacchiacca and Sogliani. These copies are of course a witness to the popularity of our Anonimo as late as 1530 or 1540.

AMICO DI SANDRO

Hanfstaengl Photo.]

THE ADORATION OF THE MAGI

" Story of Esther," which once upon a time decorated the four sides of a *cassone*. A few years ago they were still united in Casa Torrigiani at Florence. Now *schmutzgetreue* copies take the place of these, as they do of all the other masterpieces which once adorned that palace. The original panels by our Anonimo have been scattered to east and to west. The finest of them, representing the first audience that Esther has of Ahasuerus, is now in the Musée Condé, at Chantilly. The one containing the second audience belongs to M. Leopold Goldchmid of Paris. The two ends, on one of which we see Haman parading Mordecai, and on the other Esther walking in her garden, have found a resting place in the Lichtenstein Collection at Vienna. As I have said, the painting of all these panels is sketchy. They are dashed off, if you will, but never has a tale been told with lovelier grace and greater charm. Our Anonimo was improvising, no doubt, but Calliope and Aglae helped him.

All these panels are ascribed to Filippino, and according to Signor Cavalcaselle are very early works. True, were they by Filippino they would have to be regarded as belonging to his earliest years. But they are not by him. Never in his indisputable pictures does Filippino show sign of possessing such a magical gift for telling a tale ; never has he this free, careless touch ; he is never so brilliant and spirited.

On the contrary, Filippino is always more laboured, more in earnest, and he arrived at more serious—although scarcely happier—results. Even in the forms, mannerisms, or at all events in the types, where, if ever, a painter should reveal himself, we find in all the manifold motives, and in the numerous figures contained in these four paintings, but two touches which might to the competent student, to the one who had learned to distinguish clearly between painter and painter, recall Filippino. These two items are the ribbons streaming out from the baldachin of the thrones in both the long panels, and, in the one belonging to M. Goldchmid, the head of the man coming through the arch on the left. With our Anonimo, on the other hand, the points of contact are too many to be enumerated. Let us, however, note a few of the most significant.

I have already spoken of the richly golden tone, the sketchy execution, the folds of the draperies in these panels as showing an advance upon the "Adoration" and the "Stories of Virginia and Lucretia." But the identity of hand is unmistakable. We have found in all these works the same types, but in the Esther panels we have besides noted a return to certain faces that either we know our Author to have used, or that we can infer him to have used in the earliest stages of his career. And this need not surprise us, for the law of the mind is that we all tend to return to those habits which we formed in our youngest years. In the Chantilly panel, Esther conducted away from the audience chamber is, without being a direct copy of Filippo, the most Filippesque figure that we have yet found in our Anonimo. The two women of her train have faces, rather square, with broad cheeks, that suggest Verrocchio—faces, by the bye, of a type never quite paralleled in Filippino's authenticated works. Very close to Fra Filippo again, closer even than are the Turin and Lothian pictures, is the "Mordecai and Haman." The draperies throughout reveal the painter who learned from Fra Filippo how to draw them, and who then modified them under Botticelli's influence, and under the impulsion of his own improviser's way. Nowhere

THE STORY OF ESTHER

[Lichtenstein Gallery, Vienna.

ESTHER

else is our Anonimo's architecture done with such love for it, and he loses no opportunity of introducing his openings, seen aslant with the light coming through them. In short, there can be no legitimate doubt that these Esther panels are by the author of all the other pictures which we have been discussing here.[1]

Continuing the survey, in chronological order, of our painter's works, the pictures which next meet us are a " Nativity" in the palace at Meinigen ; a " Madonna with the Infant John " which passed, at the sale of Lady Eastlake's collection, into the National Gallery ; and a " Madonna with St. Francis and a Donor," recently added to the National Gallery at Buda-Pesth, all ascribed to Filippino. In the first of these we see the Madonna and an angel adoring the infant Christ. They are in a splendid portico through the arches of which we look out upon a charming and gay landscape. It is a work of the same delicacy and vivacity of feeling as the " Esther " panels. In the National Gallery painting the Madonna is seen from the knees up, standing behind a parapet against the landscape. She looks down upon the Child whom she holds in her arms, and the little Baptist in profile looks up at Him. The colour is glowing and golden, as is to be expected of our Anonimo in the later years of his apparently brief career. The types recall both his earliest and his latest years. The little John has the characteristic features of most of the faces in the various *cassone* pictures, and in the " Adoration." The

---

[1] This is perhaps the most convenient place to speak of a little " Tobias " to which, when this volume was already in press, my attention was drawn by Mr. Herbert Horne. With the picture itself I have no acquaintance, but its fortunate owner, Mr. Robert Benson, has been good enough to send me a photograph. Of its colour I cannot speak, but the forms, types and drawing of this exquisite work, point clearly to its having been painted at the same time as the " Esther " panels just discussed.

Child suggests the same works. The Madonna, however, although she has the rather turned-up nose found later, yet harks back to the quasi-Verrocchiesque types of our Anonimo's earliest paintings. Indeed, there is much in this National Gallery picture to remind us of the last of his Madonnas that we studied—Mrs. Austen's. A period of some five or six years has intervened, and our painter in his rapid course has travelled far, yet if you look carefully at the two panels you will be surprised to find how much in common they still retain.

The drawing and modelling of the eyebrows, the eyelids, and the mouth in the Madonna's face is almost identical in both pictures. The steep shoulders in both should be noted. The action of the Baptist in the one is singularly like the angel's in the other. The vase on the parapet has changed but little, and holds the same almost metallic flowers. The draperies in the later work are still conspicuously Filippesque, with large, looped or sweeping folds—so very different, by the way, from those of Filippino, at once heavier and more chopped. The Madonna's left hand takes us back to another work, to the Turin " Archangels" where the left hands of Tobias and of Gabriel are of this indentical kind. The rough painting of the hair we find at all times. Thus, the National Gallery " Madonna " with its points of resemblance to both the earlier and more recent works of our Anonimo, is like a clamp helping to hold them together in the bond of identical authorship. It will assist us in attaching to the same group still further works. But first just a word about the Buda-Pesth picture (Reproduced in " Zeitschrift für Bildende Kunst," Dec. 1897, p. 65). It is a charming painting, with the Madonna sitting in a flowered meadow. In type she is even earlier than the National Gallery Madonna.

MADONNA AND CHILD

MADONNA AND CHILD

The folds are large and of a severely Filippo-Botti-
cellesque character. She wears the little cape that the
Madonna has on in the Santa Maria Nuova picture
of the Uffizi. But the Child, the forms of the landscape, and the tone point to the present period.

Somewhat but not much later than the three pictures of which I have now spoken come a " Madonna" in Berlin (No. 82), and a " Nativity" in the
Galleria Ferroni, now exhibited in the Cenacolo
di Foligno (No. 100) at Florence. The Berlin Madonna is described by Signor Cavalcaselle ("Storia,"
vii., 107) as "feeble and somewhat mannered, probably the work of some pupil" of Filippino's.
"Feeble and somewhat mannered" it may be, but
its connection with Filippino is remote. Here,
where our Anonimo already seems in decline, he
returns more than ever to his earliest types and
practices. The Madonna is broad-faced and almost
Verrocchiesque. Her nose and mouth have the
indecision that we noted in his first pictures. Even
the hand (the one holding the book) is strikingly like
the Madonna's hand in his very first work, the one
at Naples. The shoulders are, as usual, steep ; the
folds are rare and summary ; and on a parapet is a
vase with the usual metallic flowers. As for the
Florence " Nativity," it is a charming work of exquisite blonde tone. It is ascribed to Filippino,
and the last edition of the Cicerone speaks of it as
by this master, and as "a fine early work close to
Fra Filippo." That it is nevertheless by our
Anonimo is too obvious—for such as have followed
me thus far—to need proof. A charming little
picture containing two flying angels, belonging to
Count Gregori Stroganoff of Rome, dates from the
same period.

These works, executed in every probability no

later than 1485, are in point of date the last that
can with perfect safety be attached to the group that
we have been studying.   But the pictures I have
thus far enumerated are by no means the only ones
which belong here.   There are a number of which
I have not the space to write,[1] and yet others of
which I have purposely avoided mention until this
point—a series of portraits.

Like most of the sacred and legendary subjects of
this group, these portraits also pass as Botticelli's,
or Ghirlandajo's, or Filippino's.   With Filippino
their connection is slight, and to Botticelli they are,
as we might expect, inferior both in sentiment and
in execution.

The earliest of these is the half-length female
figure known as "Esmeralda Bandinelli," which
belonged to the late Mr. Constantine Ionides of
Brighton.   She is seen full face, standing in a narrow
hall, her hair crimped and puffed over the temples,
her right hand touching a pillar, her left resting on
her right side.   Ascribed to Botticelli, this is nevertheless a highly characteristic work by our Anonimo,
dating from those years when he was most dependent
on Sandro.   This is established by everything in
the picture.   The drawing and the modelling are
exactly as in Mrs. Austen's "Madonna." The mouth
and nose, and even the eyes, have that peculiar indecision with which we now are well acquainted.
The perspectives are steep—note the bad drawing
of the base of the capital—and light streams through
the opening.   The folds of the draperies are, so to
speak, foamy.   The tone is blonde, with the hair
amber-coloured, and the flesh golden.   In fine, it is

---

[1] For a list of the pictures belonging to this group see the
second edition of my "Florentine Painters," under "Amico di
Sandro."

[*Victoria and Albert Museum.*

PORTRAIT OF ESMERALDA BANDINELLI

AMICO DI SANDRO

TWO ANGELS

a most unmistakable work by our Anonimo dating from about 1476.

Two or three years later he must have painted the well-known bust of "Giuliano de' Medici" in the Morelli Collection at Bergamo (No. 83). Here also everything recalls our Anonimo, the drawing, the modelling, the perspective, the colour, and the quality —so inferior to Sandro's own.[1] It is even inferior— owing perhaps to its not having been done from the life—to our painter when at his best, certainly inferior to such a splendid work as the male bust in the Filangieri Collection (No. 1506bis, ascribed to Ghirlandajo) at Naples. In this panel the type of face is not unlike Giuliano's, is close shaven, and seen full, behind a parapet, on which the hand rests. Behind him is a window, drawn with all our Anonimo's tricks of perspective, through which is seen a bit of highly characteristic landscape. The modelling of the face is as close as may be to that of Mrs. Austen's "Madonna," and the mouth is as in "Esmeralda Bandinelli." The tone is blonde and golden. The shade of orange on the sleeve, and its folds, are very indicative of our master, and occur in his other works frequently, but particularly in the "Esther" panels. In quality, both as painting and as interpretation, this Filangieri portrait marks our Anonimo's highest reach, and although criticism may not tolerate even slight errors of judgment, yet there is much to be said in excuse of those who would ascribe this work to Botticelli himself.

Three female profiles next demand our attention. One is the famous "Bella Simonetta" in the Pitti

---

[1] Morelli believed it to be an authentic Botticelli, and a mingling of conservatism and carelessness made me admit it into the list of Botticelli's works in the first edition of my "Florentine Painters."

(No. 353). The attribution of this awkward profile to Botticelli may already be regarded as lapsed, and indeed no serious critic who looks at the gawkiness of the figure, and the timidity of the execution, will think of Sandro as its real author. Yet it is by no means without merits of its own. There is a certain simplicity to the contours which is almost captivating, and the modelling is not without refinement. I ascribe this work to our Anonimo for many reasons difficult to state in brief, but chiefly because of the drawing, the modelling, and the colour, because of the folds, and because of the lighting and perspective of the opening. The other of these profiles is in the Lindenau Museum at Altenburg, and is far more interesting. It is of a young woman of about five-and-twenty, who faces to left, looking out through a narrowish opening. Her right hand rests on the window, and her left on a wheel. This symbol, the palm and the halo, make it not improbable that the lady was named Catherine—for there can be no question that we have to do with a portrait—and a comparison of the profile with medals (unfortunately later in date) of Caterina Sforza makes it not impossible that this is the person represented.[1] This portrait has recently, with small show of reason, been attributed to Sandro. It really is by our Anonimo. The contours are as in the " Simonetta," with the same hard line to the absurdly narrow neck. The modelling goes with the same work. The hand with the palm is exactly like Esmeralda's. And here again we have his characteristic openings, perspective and lighting, with a landscape that more

[1] See Professor Schmarsow in " Festschrift zu Ehren des Kunst-historischen Instituts zu Florenz," Leipzig, A. G. Liebeskind, p. 182. Reproduced in the " Gazette de Beaux Arts," September, 1897.

[*Morelli Collection, Bergamo.*

PORTRAIT OF GIULIANO DE' MEDICI

LA BELLA SIMONETTA

or less recalls most of our Anonimo's pictures, even
to the trees, dark and spotty against the sky, standing in a river valley of vague outlines. As for the
colour, it is now, thanks to the restorer, more like a
Mainardi than a Botticelli, but this would lead us
to suspect that originally it must have been very
blonde.

The third profile belongs to Prince Trivulzio of
Milan, and is of a character and quality so like the
" Bella Simonetta " that a glance reveals the identity
of authorship. The lady represented is more attrac-
tive, but as a work of art it is less striking.

The only other works by our painter which I shall
mention are two further portraits, male busts. The
less interesting is the one of an alert, spirited youth
in the Lichtenstein Collection at Vienna. He wears
a red cap, a coat of our painter's favourite deep
mauve, and has brown hair carelessly and coarsely
done, as was our Anonimo's wont. The drawing
and the modelling, the opening and the perspective,
are characteristic. The Louvre head (No. 1663),
(Photo. Braun) is a much finer achievement. It is
again the bust of a smooth-cheeked young man
with a rather *retroussé* nose, and crooked mouth—
both features of our painter's predilection—seen
against an opening similar, more or less, to those
that we have found in the other portraits of this
series. Once upon a time I was inclined to regard
it as Filippino's, and others have ascribed it to
Botticelli. But that it is our Anonimo's is proved
not only by the details to which I already have
referred, but by the modelling and colour as well.[1]

---

[1] In Muxel's catalogue of the Leuchtenberg collection at St.
Petersburg there is reproduced the bust of a youngish man (53
S. II.) ascribed to Masaccio, which must be by our Anonimo.
My friend, Mr. William Rankin, one of the ablest connoisseurs of

II.

Each of the pictures which we have been discussing, taken separately, might perhaps produce no further impression than that of a more or less enigmatic problem to be solved in connection with Botticelli or Filippino. But studied together we derive from them a sense of a distinct artistic personality, neither so gifted nor so deep as Sandro's, more fascinating certainly, but not so serious as Filippino's. This person has a lightness of touch, a charm of colour and tone, a vivacity of sentiment —qualities in a measure suggesting Watteau— which seldom graced the younger and relatively more laborious painter. From him our Anonimo is more easily distinguishable than from Sandro. All through his career, which, as we have seen, seems to have ended about 1485, he remained the imitator of Sandro, very close at first, and then less, but always so near that most of his better works, even the last, pass under the greater painter's name. Yet, as will have been noted, the ring of these attributions never sounded quite true, even to those who made them, and great indecision has reigned with regard to them. Considering our Anonimo's close following upon Sandro, in default of a well-established historical name for him, we shall do well to call him AMICO DI SANDRO, for whatever were his relations in real life to Botticelli—an imitator is not always a friend!—in art, he was Sandro's companion.[1]

my acquaintance, tells me that yet another portrait by the same hand is to be found in the collection of Mr. Johnson, of Philadelphia, there ascribed to Botticelli.

[1] He probably was somewhat younger, and may first have met him when they both were apprentices of Fra Filippo Lippi, for, as

BUST OF A YOUTH

We may not leave Amico di Sandro without discussing, no matter how briefly, what was his relation
to Filippino, and whether it be not possible to connect him with one of the many names—*nomen
praeterea nihil*—which bare record has transmitted
to us. Filippino, it has always been assumed, was
Botticelli's pupil. That this is true on the whole,
I would not dispute, but Botticelli alone does not
account for Filippino, neither for his types, nor for
his draperies, nor for his tendency towards a bright
or golden tone of colouring. It is because there
actually does exist a certain resemblance in all these
respects between his works and Amico's later paintings that so many of these have been mistaken for
Filippino's, or for works of his following. Some of
them show an actual decline of power, and for that
reason only, have, like the Berlin "Madonna," been
declared to be late works of Filippino, or even of
his school. We, however, have seen that if they
were Filippino's at all they would have to be
regarded as his early efforts. But we have avoided
this absurdity by realizing clearly that they are the
product of quite a distinct artist—an artist who
developed his own style with relative rapidity, yet
step by step. And despite the resemblances existing
between Filippino and Amico, their purposes were
different. At bottom Filippino was a painstaking,
almost academic artist, with a strong tendency toward what the Italians call "Seicentismo"—senti-
mentality in feeling, and the baroque in form. There
is nothing of that in Amico, who, whether grave or
gay, is a "Quattrocentist," and always a "Quattrocentist": with nothing that is already Sodoma, with
nothing at all that prefigures the late Bolognese.

we recollect, we have again and again found direct traces of
Filippo's influence in Amico.

To explain the likeness then between Amico and Filippino, I would assume that the latter, in his earlier and more sensitive years, was strongly influenced by the former. And good proof may be found in Filippino's earliest works now remaining, the Carmine frescoes, the Corsini [1] " Madonna with Angels," and the " Annunciation" at Naples. In the frescoes we are reminded of Amico, occasionally in the types, more often in the draperies, and very forcibly in the architecture, and the openings seen in perspective. As for the Corsini picture, in colour, in certain folds, and in one or two of the faces, it is so much like Amico that I hesitated for years, questioning whether it was his or Filippino's, and I was able to decide in favour of the latter only after I had clearly defined the personality of the former. The type of the Madonna is almost Verrocchiesque, such as you never again will find in Filippino, but is the rule in Amico. Here the draperies look somewhat as if drenched, and recall Amico's "Esther" panels. Even the hands (of the angels on the left) are singularly like those in Amico's Berlin " Madonna."

These are just so many proofs of Filippino's indebtedness to the elder painter. But the other angels, the Child, and the general flow of the draperies, while not at all exactly as in any other Filippino, are yet more like his than any other painter's manner. For the differences between it and Filippino's more clearly determined works, I would account by placing it several years earlier than the first dated picture—the Uffizi altar-piece of February, 1486. The Naples "Annunciation" (Sala Toscana 37, Photo. Alinari), is of somewhat later date, but again so little like Filippino's conventional manner, and so close to Amico, that I used to incline to believe it by the latter,

[1] At Florence.

while other writers have been puzzled into ascribing it to Raffaellino del Garbo. This attribution merits no attention. The highly characteristic hands and ears, the outlines, the types are decidedly Filippino's, but in colouring (the golden mauve for instance) and in the draperies it is close to Amico.[1]

Filippino, then, was certainly strongly influenced by Amico, if not actually his pupil. Even later, his type of Madonna recalls the Madonna in Amico's National Gallery " Adoration," and his male heads are tall and slim as in the man passing through a door in M. Goldchmid's panel representing " Esther's Second Audience."

It now remains for us to discuss the other question, whether Amico may not be some one of those painters who has remained a mere empty name, one of the many names in Vasari and other records, with whom no works of art are now connected. Now it is not likely, on the face of it, that no record whatever should have remained of a personality so important, consider ing what petty artists have been immortalized by Messer Giorgio. On the other hand, if a painter died young, as early as 1485 perhaps, leaving few or no works where they would have attracted constant attention, as in churches or other public places, then, by 1550, when Vasari was writing, the memory of him might have grown very dim. We have seen that Amico's career came to an end toward 1485. We have discovered no work of his *al fresco*, and of his known pictures but one or at the utmost two are of a size and kind presupposing their having been painted for places of open worship, rather than for private use.

My friend Mr. Herbert Horne, in conning the

---

[1] Filippino's early altar-piece in S. Michele at Lucca (photo. Alinari) also stands very close to Amico.

pages of Vasari, was struck by the significance of the following lines in the lives of Chimenti Camicia and Baccio Pontelli, and was kind enough to point them out to me :—" Chimenti Camicia, of whose family nothing further is known than that he was Florentine, designed for the King of Hungary, while in his service, palaces, gardens, fountains, temples, fortresses, and many other important edifices, which were executed with great care by Baccio Cellini. Finishing these works, as befitted one in love with his native town, he returned to Florence. To Baccio, however, who remained behind, he sent for the king several pictures by Berto Linaiuolo. These were considered most beautiful by the Hungarians, and were much praised by the King. As for Berto (I will say just this much about him) after having painted beautifully a number of pictures which may be seen in the houses of many townspeople, he died at the very moment of maturity, bringing to nought the expectations he had aroused."[1]

Now the Chimenti and Baccio here mentioned are known to have been in Hungary in 1480. The Berto referred to as having died just when attaining full maturity, must, in 1480, or just later, have been already sufficiently perfected in his art to make his pictures valued. This would agree excellently well with our Amico who, soon after 1480, was painting such delightful things as the " Story of Esther." Amico also, we concluded, must have died at the very point of his maturity.[2] That a person like Amico must also have roused considerable expectation we can readily believe, and like Amico, Berto seems to have

[1] Vasari, ed. Sansoni, ii., p. 651.
[2] If, by the way, his career stopped in 1485, he yet may have been born no later than 1450, which would have given him ample time to be the pupil of Filippo Lippi.

painted chiefly for private houses. Vasari's Berto and
our Amico coincide very well therefore, in date no less
than in condition. Nor is there aught to make against
an hypothesis of their identity. On the contrary, there
is just a point in its favour. In 1488 Filippino sent
some pictures to the King of Hungary.[1] The connection between Filippino and Amico-Berto we have
established. What more natural than to suppose that
after Berto's death the King transferred his patron-
age from the master to the pupil, or follower ?

Amico di Sandro may therefore be the historical
Berto Linaiuolo. But, as until further proof appears,
this can be no more than an hypothesis, and as the
real name of Berto Linaiuolo[2] is neither more familiar
nor more pleasant, I prefer to call our Anonimo
" Amico di Sandro."

[1] Vasari, ed. Sansoni, iii., p. 467.
[2] Berto is mentioned almost in Vasari's terms in "Antonio Billi"
as well as in the "Anonimo Magliabecchiano." See Carl Fry's
"Antonio Billi," p. 53, and "Codice Magliabecchiano," p. 102.
Both, Berlin, 1892.

CERTAIN COPIES AFTER LOST ORIGINALS BY GIORGIONE.

So copious are the materials at hand for the study of the Italian Masters that scarcely an attempt has been made to apply to them the methods of research without which the bent of Greek art would have remained entirely unknown to us. I mean the kind of research which, proceeding with the aid of literary reference, and of copies and adaptations, ultimately arrives at some notion of what the great masterpieces of Greek sculpture were like. More than a mere notion such enquiry can never yield; for even when we are certain that at last we know the exact shape and proportions of a lost statue by Pheidias or Polycleitus, our knowledge must stop there, remaining mere knowledge. To go further, to pass from the shape to the intimate, mystic beauty, without which shape has scarcely more to give to the refined sense than shapelessness—to endow the copy or adaptation with a portion even of the loveliness with which an original by a Greek master must have glowed, it is necessary that we should be acquainted with original works by these masters. But where may such be found? Where may one see a marble carved and moulded by Pheidias's own hand?

Yet, archeologists do not despair. Legions of them are incessantly at work, following out the slightest indication, as unflagging as the Renaissance searchers after the philosopher's stone. What if their results

often bear more likeness to the discoveries of the
self-deluded alchemist than to exploits of the man
of science ?   What though their gold frequently is
dross ?   At times, it *is* gold, and that suffices.

But we who study the art of the Renaissance have
much surer ground to walk upon, and if only we have
learned to use our eyes, our imaginations and our
reasoning faculties as the discipline of art demands,
we can attain to results of a certainty and tangibility
almost impossible in Classical Archeology.

It is my intention to speak of a few copies after
lost originals by Giorgione, the great master whose
works have grown rarer than those of any other Renaissance artist of importance.   Yet rare though he
has become, we possess works of his of an authenticity that no competent critic will dispute, and works,
too, which represent every phase of his brief but
manifold career.   Once agreed that a given picture
must be a copy after a lost original by Giorgione,
those of us who have the capacity for breathing artistic life into the lifelessness of a copy (and without
such capacity the critic is far worse than useless)
can have no difficulty in assimilating the copy to the
style of some one at least of the existing originals,
and of endowing it, in our mental vision, with the
exact kind, if not the full quality, of the beauty its
prototype must have had when it left Giorgione's
hand.   " To him that hath it shall be given."   And
just because Giorgione, as compared with any great
Greek master, has so much, it is possible to give him
still more, and a more that is worth while, for we are
in a position to be able to translate copies after him
back into almost the pristine beauty of originals.

I.

How shall we agree that such and such a picture must be a copy after a Giorgione? Rather than describe in the abstract the method of research, I will allow the method to reveal itself in the course of this article. Naturally, one takes for granted an acquaintance with Venetian painting sufficient to know that a given picture is in style closer to one master than to another. No one thus equipped can fail to note the Giorgionesque character of the David with the head of Goliath in the Imperial Gallery at Vienna (No. 21). The broad forehead, the distance between the eyes, the mouth, then the oval of the face, and finally the hair, are all so many countersigns of Giorgione's riper ideal of the youthful visage. The conception is no less characteristic of the master. He makes no attempt to present a youth who could have performed a grandly heroic deed, nor does he endeavour to depict the young hero's exultation over his astounding victory. The head before us is idyllic, dreamy, the head of a Daphnis whose fingers should be toying with Chloe's lovely curls. The brave show of arms and armour, the grizzly giant's head, are so much mere painting, so much mere labelling—they do not really belong to the character the artist has given to the young hero.

Now for the competent critic there can be no doubt that this picture is either an original Giorgione or a copy after him. Mere inspection should reveal this. But from people who dare not trust the testimony of their eyes unless it be guided by a document, it would be asking too much to require them to believe in the attribution of a picture without some historical certificate. It is true no notary

COPY AFTER GIORGIONE

DAVID

[Vienna Gallery.

has left an attestation of his presence while Giorgione was painting this picture. But such proof—and it is the only *documentary* proof that could make a claim to being adequate—has never been given regarding any picture; and in default of better, Vasari has been agreed upon as a sufficiently respectable sponsor.

Well, Vasari, in his "Life of Giorgione," speaks of a picture by this master that he saw in the palace of the Patriarch of Aquileia. He describes it as " a David with a shock of hair, such as used to be worn in those days, down to the shoulders, lively and coloured, so as to seem flesh and blood. He has an arm and the chest covered with armour, and holds the head of Goliath." [1]

Granting, what no one will dispute, that the David at Vienna is very Giorgionesque, allowing that Vasari's description applies to this picture as closely as words ever can apply, we must conclude that this self-same work, or a replica thereof, was seen by Vasari, and by him, and great Venetian tradition, ascribed to Giorgione.

This much then is settled. The question remains open still whether the panel before us is an original or a copy; and that is a question which scarcely any kind of document conceivable, certainly none that ever has been adduced, can settle. We are forced to fall back upon the merits of the picture, to decide whether these are on a level with the quality of works by Giorgione now beyond dispute, to determine whether the execution is adequate to the conception.

The Vienna "David" is exceedingly hard and coarse in execution. The head of the slain giant is indeed lifeless, not with the mere lifelessness of

[1] Vasari, ed. Sansoni, iv., p. 93.

death, but with the far worse corruption of the thing
which never had life. The armour, the sword, have
none of that glimmer which Giorgione could give
them, as if the sun's rays falling upon them had
been shivered into sparks of gold. In the young
hero's face, the mouth and the nose could scarcely
be more wretchedly drawn, the eyes and the hair
more mechanically. Giorgione could not have
painted a picture in execution so deplorable.

Fortunately we are so situated that we not only
can be perfectly sure that the Vienna "David" (in
its present condition, at least) is not Giorgione's,
but we can obtain an idea of the exact quality
that his original must have had. At Hampton
Court there is "A Shepherd with a Flute"* which
can be by no other painter than Giorgione. The
head of the "David" and the head of the "Shepherd" are, in everything but quality, identical—but
in quality what a difference! How sweet is the
mouth in the Hampton Court picture; how sensitive
the nostrils; how the eyes glow under the smooth
broad brow!—and the hair has the magic of a
summer sunset seen through a long stretch of forest.

The head of the "David" in the original of the
Vienna picture could have been no less beautiful.
Imagine it as beautiful; give Goliath the power
Giorgione surely gave him, the armour its sparkle,
and you have brought to life again something so
precious as a masterpiece by Giorgione.[1]

---

[1] Professor Wickhoff assures me that if this panel were cleaned
from its disfiguring restoration and repainting, it would turn out
to be not a copy at all, but Giorgione's very original.

---

* See p. 142.

From an Old Engraving.]

THE FINDING OF PARIS

II.

None of the other copies of which I shall speak can be treated with such complete satisfaction as the "David." Even where there will appear enough proof to convince the competent that a given picture is a copy after a lost Giorgione, I shall not be able to offer them again such perfect aid for translating the copy back into an original. They will have to use their artistic imagination. If they have no such artistic faculty, all the learning and all the penetration in the world will, alas! not make them competent critics.

We need not stop long over the picture at Buda-Pesth, which Morelli identified as a fragment of Giorgione's "Birth of Paris," seen in 1525 by the Anonimo Morelliano in the house of Taddeo Contarini.[1] This discovery is of such importance in itself that no generous person will grudge Morelli the enthusiasm which blinded his eyes to the fact that the Esterhazy fragment can be but a copy— and a very poor copy—of the lost original. Giorgione could not have painted figures so lifeless, so stupid, so uncouth as these two shepherds. There is not a redeeming touch of vivacity in the entire canvas. But this is a case where one must be thankful for small favours.[2]

[1] I. Lermolieff, "Die Galerien zu München und Dresden," p. 284.
[2] The interesting question arises whether this fragment is part of the entire work which was in the collection of the Archduke Leopold Wilhelm of the Netherlands, or is independent of it. If independent, then there is a chance that the picture in the Archduke's collection was the original, and that some day it may reappear. Of course, no decision can be made from the double translation of the picture, first into the forms of Teniers, and then

III.

In the Hermitage (No. 112) there is a full-length figure of radiant beauty (judging from the photograph) in which Morelli discerned a possible Giorgione. Tall and graceful, but not quite so slender as the women in Giorgione's earliest pictures, " The Trial of Moses" and " The Judgment of Solomon," at the Uffizi, Judith stands majestic, yet soft and idyllic, reclining against a tree. Her right hand rests lightly on the handle of her gleaming sword. Her bare foot rests with equal lightness on the head of Holofernes lying in the lush grass. Even less than in the " David" is there a feeling of horror or of triumph. The placid air of a summer noontide in a park-like glen among the Euganean hills is breathed in this idyl. The lovely lady in the sweetness of her heart toys with a sword for its beauty, and she looks at the head with as gracious a smile as if it were a fragrant flower at her feet.

It would take a poet of the highest order to convey to the full the impression of the St. Petersburg " Judith." Yet regarded as painting, rather than as poetry, I fear it can be nothing but a copy. Surely Giorgione would not have painted arms so lax, hands so lifeless; draperies so devoid of lineal quality; Giorgione would not have painted a leg so much like a stuffed stocking; Giorgione certainly would not have drawn so badly as this head of Holofernes is drawn. Look at Judith's own head. It is far from satisfactory, but how superior as execution to the rest of the picture,—and this betrays the copyist as nothing else. The head interested him

into those of the engraver, which we find in the "Theatrum Pictoricum."

more than the rest, as is always the case with people
whose appreciation of art is feeble, and he copied it
with especial care. A real artist, on the other hand,
is of the same quality throughout. An excellent
and invaluable copy is this " Judith " of the Hermitage, but only a copy.

IV.

The original of the " Judith " must have been
painted somewhat later than the Castelfranco
Madonna. With this sublime figure " Judith " has
much in common, yet seems maturer, less austere,
nay, more opulent, more pagan. I would now speak
of a picture which I believe to be of about the same
date and tendency. It is a Cassone panel in the
Lochis Collection at Bergamo, and has attracted
little, if any, attention. It represents the story of
Orpheus and Eurydice. In a landscape of idyllic
charm, we see to the left Eurydice, a lovely Venetian
figure, fleeing from the reptile. In the background
to the right are the flaming towers of the house of
Hades. In the middle distance we see Eurydice
turning back to the sombre fires, while Orpheus
whirls away in despair.

Where everything is so Giorgionesque, how shall
one speak of it to those who do not see the relation
of this fascinating panel to Giorgione? Let me ask
who else ever assimilated Greek myth to the spirit of
a later age, as it has been done here? I speak not
only of the completeness, but of the refinement and
charm of the process. Who but Giorgione had the
gift of harmonizing landscape and figures into one
such lovely strain as this picture gives us? The flaming walls of Hades, the small figures in the middle

distance, the movement of Eurydice, the graceful tree blowing over her, are all so many touches which suggest Giorgione, and none but Giorgione. Nor do they in combination call up this great master in the vague only; on the contrary, the "Orpheus and Eurydice" is an instant reminder of that panel so charming even in its ruin, the "Apollo and Daphne" of the Seminario at Venice—a picture first seriously attributed to Giorgione by Morelli, and since then accepted as such by most competent critics. The feeling and the treatment in both are so identical that to speak further of their resemblance to each other would simply be repeating what I already have said of the Lochis picture.

But a careful comparison of the two will reveal not only that the last-named panel does not quite attain to the supreme touch of the "Apollo and Daphne," but also that in slight, and, to the listless eye, almost imperceptible details, the "Orpheus and Eurydice" departs from the forms peculiar to Giorgione. The head of Eurydice, for instance, has not quite Giorgione's cranium. The folds of her drapery are even less strictly Giorgione's. Indeed, is it not here where one is tempted to perceive the hand of one of Giorgione's more gifted followers, namely, Cariani?[1] Nay, a careful inspection of the panel leads one to observe Cariani's touch elsewhere, particularly in the actual handling.

Now pleasant, and even at times delightful, as Cariani is, he scarcely would be worth the study required to know him well, was it not for the service such study can do us in cases similar to this. The elegant dilettante who enjoys what he considers to be great masterpieces, and them only, is of course satis-

[1] I owe this very interesting suggestion to my friend Dr. Gustavo Frizzoni.

COPY AFTER GIORGIONE

ORPHEUS AND EURYDICE

[*Lochis Gallery, Bergamo.*

GIORGIONE

Anderson Photo.] [Seminario, Venice.

APOLLO AND DAPHNE

fied with his own enjoyment and cares to go no further. But a serious student can never stop until he
knows well all the followers of the great artist, even
to the lowest rank ; for even the lowest may reveal
to us some precious trait of which abhorrent accident
has deprived us in the extant works of the master.
Or, as in the case before us, the follower may have
copied the great painter, yet being, as was Cariani,
not without mannerisms if not a style of his own,
we must know the ways of the smaller man so well
that we can at once scale them off, leaving bare if
not the original, something at all events nearer to
the original. Then if we were highly gifted artists
ourselves, we could replace detail for detail with the
scrupulously faithful Giorgionesque, taken from some
work of nearest kin. Here it should be from the
" Apollo and Daphne."

But as we are not artists we must be satisfied with
a reconstruction appealing to the mind's eye only.
As for me, even that is reward more than sufficient.

V.

The so-called " Historical Method " has in our
century been the chief formative principle in all intellectual pursuits. We owe it so great a debt of
gratitude that perhaps it were ungracious to say that,
in art at least, it has not been altogether an unmixed
blessing. Yet I must say it. The blind habit in-
duced by the Historical Method has tended to turn
students to the question of mere origins, without due
consideration whether in art in general, or at all
events in a particular artist, that question be really
of dominant significance. This is neither the place
nor the occasion to institute that revolt against the

Historical Method which we shall have to pass through if, in art study, perhaps above all other studies, we are not to fall into a new Scholasticism, or rather Byzantinism.

The worst effect of the Historical Method has been that, concentrating attention overpoweringly on the question *how* the artist came to be what he was, it overshot its own intention and ended by taking only a feeble and languid interest in what the artist *actually was*, particularly in his more independent, more mature phases. In Titian, for instance, this method has led to an exaggerated interest in and appreciation of those earlier works in which, delightful though he is, to the more refined sense he seems to aspire after rather than to attain to Giorgione's greatness. In the case of Giorgione the same method has led to his being quite misunderstood. Even those who have a scientific acquaintance with this great master's maturer works have remained untouched by them, and go on thinking of Giorgione as the refinedly idyllic or solemnly lyrical painter of the " Trial of Moses" and of the Castalfranco Madonna.

But in the later years of his pathetically brief life Giorgione, rapidly growing out of mere refinement and daintiness, was fast attaining to a power and magnificence of the kind that Titian did not reach until he had passed his seventieth birthday. The power and splendour of the old Titian or even of Rubens had been all but attained by Giorgione at his death. But Giorgione added to it a refinement and a distinction that was never reached by Rubens, and scarcely Titian himself.

To those, however, who have no adequate acquaintance with all the subtlest ins and outs of Venetian art in the first decades of the Cinquecento, this phase of

Giorgione's career has remained so unappreciated, has so little revealed itself as the inevitable evolution of a great mind and an even greater art, that they have doubted the attributions one after the other of all the grand works of this, Giorgione's grandest style. The "Knight of Malta" has been questioned; the "Fête Champetre" has been questioned; absurdest of all, even the Dresden "Venus"—the discovery of which ranks as an achievement with the greatest feats of our times—even this doubly and triply unquestionable masterpiece has been questioned. And, most extraordinary of all, the work which, despite the incompleteness in which Giorgione left it, the incompetent hands that have tampered with it, the ruin that it has been subjected to, remains one of Giorgione's greatest achievements, the work in which, without ceasing to be himself, he comes nearest to the imaginativeness of Leonardo and the gigantic vigour of Michelangelo, that work —of course I refer to the "St. Mark saving Venice from the Demons"—has in Venice itself, where of all places Giorgione should be known, met with so little recognition that in the recent rehanging of the gallery, this masterpiece has been placed in the corner of a corridor where, even if it were not in cross lights, one cannot sufficiently stand back from it to see it.

I insist so much on this point because the two copies I shall now speak of are on the whole even farther away from the "Trial of Moses" and "Judgment of Solomon" than the works I have just mentioned. They are even more like Rubens—but Rubens was never so profound. They are not likely therefore to find a ready acceptance on the part of such critics as have the penetrating sagacity to doubt the "Fête Champêtre" or the Dresden "Venus."

The first of the two pictures, both portraits, which I am thus, perhaps over-elaborately, introducing, is a half-length figure of a Venetian gentleman that used to belong to the late Mr. Henry Doetsch.[1]   Between a parapet, heightened to one side, and a wall, with an opening on the Doge's Palace and the Bridge of Sighs, we see the powerful bust of a Venetian Noble. He is not quite in profile to the left.   His hair is in a net as in all Giorgione's male busts.   His firmly clenched right hand rests on a book, which in turn rests on the parapet.

The face is one of those which seem to brood in melancholy over energies their owners know not what to do with, while proudly conscious of power and full of determination.   It is like the haunting face of that youth at Buda-Pesth—the portrait in which Morelli again identified, if somewhat timidly, the hand of Giorgione—a character which fascinates the mind and yet repels the sympathies.   And to represent a person as unsympathetic, as consumed with self, as are the head I am now introducing and the Esterhazy portrait, requires the very greatest of artists— an artist at least as great as Velasquez.

People will smile and say, " Of course, Velasquez now is the name, and so by hook or by crook the critic who has exhausted his paltry pouch of phrases will try to compare even Giorgione with the impersonal, impassive, disinterested Spaniard."   Yet is the comparison so far-fetched ?   As interpretation is there not a startling likeness between the spirit of the two portraits by Giorgione of which I am speaking and the spirit of the various likenesses of Phillip IV. and of Olivarez by Velasquez ?   And it is not only in feeling that Giorgione here has

[1] What has become of it since the scattering of this extraordinary, if most unequal collection, is unknown to me.

COPY AFTER GIORGIONE

[From the Doetsch Sale, London.

PORTRAIT OF A GENTLEMAN

travelled so far away from his earlier, better-known self. His sense of structure has increased apace; and his tone has approached those exquisite harmonies in cool gray, the mastery over which makes Velasquez the very greatest, perhaps, of colourists.

But it still remains for me to prove that the picture of the Doetsch Collection is more than merely Giorgionesque, that it is really a copy after a lost Giorgione. I would ask, to begin with, who else could have created a masterpiece such as the original of this picture must have been—for that it is a copy of something vastly better is, to the discerning eye, amply proved by the discrepancy between the conception and the execution? Titian, who in his earlier years follows Giorgione so closely, betrays in no work even plausibly ascribed to him, a style of portraiture at all of this kind. The author of this portrait, if not Giorgione himself, would have to be some conscious imitator like Licinio or Beccaruzzi. But these petty painters could imitate only, and not create—and the Doetsch portrait was the work of a creator. Licinio, as in the portrait belonging to Louisa Lady Ashburton, can well produce a crude, obvious resemblance to Giorgione, but to infuse spirit and splendour into a work was a task beyond him.

The student who has an adequate acquaintance with Venetian painting in the epoch of Giorgione, will then, by a process of exclusion or elimination, arrive at the conviction that none but Giorgione could have created the original of the Doetsch portrait. A comparison with one or two works the authenticity of which is beyond reasonable question, will bear out this conclusion. In the first place, with its next of kin, the Esterhazy portrait—the same type of cranium, the identical dressing of the hair, the same broad brow, the same sweep of the hair over it, and an almost identical treatment of the mouth and eyes. Where slight differences come in, it is largely the copyist's, and not the creator's, work. Let us next compare this Doetsch portrait with the exquisite work discovered by Dr. J. P. Richter, and now *primus inter pares* among the many masterpieces of Italian art in the Museum of Berlin. Again the same cranium, the same forehead, the same slight drawing up of the sitter's left brow, and the same feeling in the mouth. Surely such identity in significant detail as the Doetsch portrait has with both these works, coupled with such identity in spirit as it has with one, added to the absence of any other possible claimant to the authorship, makes the attribution of its original to Giorgione unavoidable. And let us translate its lack of quality into the power and puissant modelling of the Esterhazy portrait, and we shall have added—for the initiated only, it is true—a masterpiece to our list of Giorgione's works.

VI.

This last work is almost in profile. Let us imagine it full face, and we shall be struck by the strong family resemblance it bears to the remaining copy after a lost Giorgione of which I promised to speak. It is the portrait of a lady in the collection of Signor Crespi at Milan. Were the original before us, I scarcely should hesitate to proclaim it the chief among Giorgione's portraits, and a masterpiece with no superior among portraits of all times and countries. It is a blessed chance that has preserved for us at

COPY AFTER GIORGIONE

PORTRAIT OF A LADY

least a copy of such a work, and a copy so excellent,
to boot.

I said just now that Signor Crespi's portrait had
a certain family resemblance to the one of the former
Doetsch Collection.   There, however, barring morphological details, the likeness ends.   In character, in
temperament, the persons were of different universes,
and in artistic conception the works are scarcely
less divergent.   François Rabelais, not as the vulgar
know him, but as he reveals himself to his nobler
votaries, an artist glowing with the purifying fires
of health, kindling into exuberant life whatsoever
he touches, the last re incarnation of Dionysus—
Rabelais then, or perhaps Shakespeare, in some divine moment between creating Titania and Falstaff,
—had either of them been a painter, might well
have painted the original of this portrait.   The
Italian lady in her health and magnificence is before
us, restlessly energetic, exuberant, full of interest,
full of warming sympathy, with a power of carrying
everything before her, a source of life and joy to all
who surround her—yet cool-headed, penetrating, and
ironical, although full of indulgence.

In so far as my poor words can express it, such is
the kind of person who looks out at us from Signor
Crespi's portrait, as she stands, visible down to the
knees, behind a parapet, part of which is so much
raised that she can rest her hand upon it.   It is a
spacious composition, fit for a personality so opulent.
A touch of great decorative effect is the profile in
grisaille on the parapet the same lady in another
phase.

So far as I know, two, and two only, attributions
have been suggested for this work. To make Licinio
its author was an idea of my own propounded years
ago when, in the heat of rediscovering this far from

insignificant painter, I was hoping to find him worthy of such a masterpiece. Further study of Licinio—and I believe I have been able to identify, between pictures and portraits, some forty of his paintings—leads me to the conclusion that such a portrait as Signor Crespi's is as much above the reach of Licinio as the flight of the eagle is above the hop of the grasshopper, and that even in the morphological details and in the handling there is, strictly speaking, nothing of his. Besides, there is such a gulf here between the conception and the execution, that while Signor Crespi's portrait remains a very good copy, it can be no more than a copy.

The other attribution would give this work to Titian, and it is the one entertained by the owner himself. Now the opinion of a collector of Signor Crespi's stamp deserves every consideration—has it not been said, " By their fruits shall ye know them ? "—and besides, the idea is on its own merits excellent and plausible. To begin with, the only other artist, besides Giorgione, who conceivably could have created this portrait is Titian, in some supreme moment, under Giorgione's inspiration. And, indeed, if we look at two of Titian's works in which he with the greatest merit wears the mantle of his just departed companion and inspirer—if we look at two of Titian's frescoes in the Scuola del Santo at Padua, we shall see what will tempt us to agree with Signor Crespi. Look at the fresco representing St. Antony, who gives speech to an infant that he may bear witness to his mother's innocence. Never again shall you find such an obvious and striking likeness to Signor Crespi's portrait as is afforded by the figure of the infant's mother in this work executed by Titian just after Giorgione's death, under the full glow of his inspiration.   Moreover, the Crespi portrait bears on the parapet the initials, T. V.

Yet, despite all this, I cannot share Signor Crespi's opinion.   As for the initials, I must confess they are puzzling.   But Giorgione's portraits at Buda-Pesth and at Berlin are also decorated with enig-matical initials, and T. V. may well represent the initials of the person represented, or the owner. There was no lack at Venice of Veniers and Ven-dramins, surely.   Besides, I can recall in Titian's earlier years no parallel to this blatant and defiant form of signature.

Without solving the mystery of these initials, we may, I think, feel free to shake ourselves loose from their bondage, and judge of the portrait by morpho-logical and qualitative considerations only.   Now the feeling for quality is not capable of demonstra-tion ; the utmost one can hope to do is to draw the attention of such as can appreciate it, to a quality which, for some reason, has escaped their notice. Well, wonderfully fine and Giorgionesque as is Titian's Paduan fresco, I personally feel in it not only a difference, but an inferiority in conception to Giorgione.   I feel neither here, nor in the Pesaro Madonna, nor even in all the sweep and opulence of the "Assunta," nor in any of Titian's works exe-cuted before, let us say, 1540, anything like the spontaneous force, the easy gift, the commanding genius which reveals itself to me in Signor Crespi's picture.   The younger Titian, as I know him—and I cannot plead ignorance—was not of a height for such an achievement.   Of course, no one would dream of ascribing it to his later years.

Above Titian in genius, copy though it be, it yet betrays a superiority to him even in execution.   As usual, the copyist has done greater justice to the face.

Now, allowing always that it is a copy and not an original we are looking at, is not this face neverthe-less modelled with more power and splendour, does it not reveal an artist with a profounder, more essential feeling for form than we shall find even in the young Titian?   So certainly it seems to me.

And now for some rather more matter-of-fact con-siderations.   Titian does not seem to have affected the raised parapet. Titian never places the fingers as they are placed here.   But these same fingers are in the very copy subtly Giorgione's. Compare them, for instance, with the fingers in the Berlin portrait. Then, look here at the broad, low brow, the sweep of the hair over the forehead—I have pointed them out again and again in the course of this article in Gior-gione's other portraits. The eye-brows and the nose should be seen in connection with the Hampton Court "Shepherd" and the Dresden "Venus." But far more subtly characteristic than all these details, yet because of its subtlety not obvious, not to be pointed out to everybody, is the intimate movement, the vibration which the great artist gives to the figure he paints. Look at the pose, the vibration of the figure in Signor Crespi's portrait, and at the same time at Giorgione's "Knight of Malta." There scarcely could be, considering the difference in the sitters, a greater likeness in pose and movement—and in my opinion there is than this no stronger proof of their being by the same painter.   After this it were vain to discuss pettier details, such, for instance, as the folds of the drapery, which, despite the greater carelessness of the copyist just here, yet remain more like Giorgione's than like that of anybody else whatsoever.

*   *   *   *   *

If, as I firmly believe, Giorgione was the author of the grand work in the Venice Academy, of which I

have spoken in the course of this article, if also he
was the author of such portraits as are preserved for
us in the copies of the Doetsch and Crespi collections,
then Giorgione not only was more than the rival of
Raphael in idyllic charm, the companion of Leonardo
in subtlety and refinement, but the equal of Melozzo
in spontaneity of conception, and, for sheer energy,
almost the peer of Michelangelo.

VENETIAN PAINTING, CHIEFLY
BEFORE TITIAN.

[At the Exhibition of Venetian Art, New Gallery, 1895.]

RARELY have I seen a catalogue so accurate as well as tactful, in its description of works of art, as the official catalogue to the Venetian Exhibition at the New Gallery. It has one and only one fault, that the attributions are, for the most part, unreliable. It is, of course, not to be reproached for this fault, since it merely gives the attributions the pictures bear in the private collections from which they come;[1] but it is clear that it needs rectification in this respect, if it is to be of value to students of pictures or to those who are interested in the history of Renaissance art. This, I think, will be readily conceded when we have examined two or three typical instances.

To Titian, for example, thirty-three paintings are ascribed. Of these, one only is actually by the master, Mr. Mond's "Madonna" (No. 244), a thoroughly characteristic work of his greatest, although latest, period. Of the thirty-two pictures that remain, a dozen and more have no connection whatever with Titian, and are either too remote

---

[1] At the head of the official catalogue it is stated : " The works are catalogued under the names given to them by the contributors. The Committee cannot be responsible for the attributions."

from our present subject or too poor to require our attention. Five are copies, of varying degrees of merit, after well known originals :—Mrs. R. H. Benson's " Daughter of Herodias " (No. 129, original in the Doria Gallery, Rome) ; M. Léon Somzée's "Venus Worship" (No. 136, original at Madrid) : Lord Cowper's " Lavinia (No. 152, original at Berlin) ; Lord Brownlow's " Magdalen " (No. 173, original in the Pitti at Florence) ; and Louisa, Lady Ashburton's little " Strozzi Girl " (No. 213, original at Berlin). Two are copies after unknown or lost originals :—Lord Malmesbury's " Lucretia " (No. 217, another version is at Hampton Court, No. 75) ; and the Duke of Westminster's copy of what must have been a splendid original, the " Duke of Urbino and his Son " (No. 257). Most of the pictures still unaccounted for are by various imitators :—Four are by Titian's clever follower, Polidoro Lanzani, the Glasgow " Holy Family " (No. 133), Captain Holford's " Holy Family " (No. 158), Sir William Farrer's " Holy Family and Two Donors " (No. 179), and Lord Battersea's " Madonna with the Infant John " (No. 227). Another so-called " Titian," Captain Holford's " Madonna and Saints " (No. 7), is by Girolamo Santacroce; another by Andrea Schiavone, Sir William Farrer's " St. Jerome " (No. 95) ; and another by Domenico Caprioli, Mme. C. de Rosenberg's " Portrait of Doge Grimani " (No. 124) ; while two further are probably the work of Francesco Beccaruzzi, Lord Powerscourt's so-called " Portrait of Politian " (No. 205), and Captain Holford's " Portrait of Doge Gritti " (No. 248). Of the two pictures that still remain unaccounted for, Captain Holford's so-called " Portrait of a Lady of the Sforza Family " (No. 156) is a fine work by Girolamo Romanino in his blond, late manner, and M. Somzée's " Portrait of a Venetian Lady" (No. 234) is by some late Veronese painter of the quality of G. Fasolo or Bernardino India.

This brief analysis shows the need there is for some emendation or supplement to the official catalogue. No other name, it is true, is so recklessly abused as Titian's, but other instances of superannuated connoisseurship are not far to seek. Eight pictures, for instance, are catalogued as by Bonafazio, although not one is genuine. Similar is the case of Paolo Veronese, to whom thirteen pictures are falsely ascribed, one of them, M. Somzée's "Christ at the House of Levi" (No. 241) being, indeed, a Tiepolesque copy of the Venetian original (as is amply proved by the spirit and technique); and we shall see later what a small proportion of real as compared with attributed Bellinis and Giorgiones there is in this exhibition.

But even aside from the abuse of famous names, the old connoisseurship was guilty of applying at random to a picture the first name that happened to suggest itself, without stopping to inquire whether the resemblance, real or fancied, was due to anything but chance. A couple of instances to the point are two pictures here attributed to Paris Bordone and Moroni respectively. The former, a so-called "Alfonzo II. d'Este and his Mistress" (No. 163, lent by Lord Malmesbury,) is really by the widely-divergent Calisto Piazza, of Lodi; while the latter, Lord Battersea's "Portrait of a Man" (No. 20), is both as art and workmanship at the opposite pole from Moroni, being in fact a work by Domenico Brusasorci, of Verona.

All these instances have, I trust, made it apparent that the person who cares to get a clear idea of the various masters whose works are exhibited here needs further guidance than is supplied by the official catalogue. To supply, so far as I am able, this necessary further guidance, particularly for the earlier masters, is the object of the following pages.

I.

The earliest Venetian here is MICHELE GIAMBONO. This artist has, heretofore, been known only by his three signed works—the polyptych in the Venice Academy (No. 3), the "Madonna," belonging to Sir F. Leighton (now in the "Old Masters" at Burlington House, No. 136), and the mosaics in the Cappella dei Mascoli of St. Mark's. These reveal him as the follower of Gentile da Fabriano, and the kinsman in art of Antonio Vivarini, Jacopo Bellini, Vittorio Pisanello, and Stefano da Zevio. But, even with these works, his artistic personality has remained very vague, and we greet with interest the small half-length figure of "St. Mark" (No. 200, lent by Mr. Ludwig Mond), which appears to be correctly ascribed to him. The forms, the drawing, and the feeling—elements wherein Giambono is less influenced by Renaissance *motifs* than any of his mates—justify this ascription, and the colouring—deeper than that of most early Venetian paintings—also points to the mosaicist as its author. It is a pity that Dr. J. P. Richter's glowing panel by the same artist is not also here, to add to our knowledge of Giambono, but I fancy that if Sir F. Leighton's

---

[1] A number of the pictures here to be discussed have been photographed by the New Gallery, and prints are to be had of its secretary. Others will be found in an album entitled "Venetian Art," published in 1895 by Blades, East, and Blades.

signed "Madonna" were placed side by side with the "Madonna" (No. 77) lent by Mr. Fairfax Murray, under the name of Stefano da Zevio, we should not long hesitate in recognizing the hand of the same master in both, so striking alike are the forms, the drawing, and the colouring. Before we can properly know Giambono, we must be able to differentiate him from his contemporaries, from Stefano da Zevio in such a work as the "Madonna" mentioned above, from Jacopo Bellini in such a picture as the "St. Crisogono," of San Trovaso at Venice[1] (sometimes ascribed to Giambono), and from Antonio Vivarini, who comes very close to him in the *predelle* (Nos. 1280-1283) in the Salles des Sept Maîtres of the Louvre (there labelled "Ecole de Gentile da Fabriano"). And until we are able so to differentiate Giambono from his compeers as to have a precise idea of his career and quality, our knowledge of the beginnings of modern painting in Venice must remain in the hazy state in which it is at present.[2]

II.

Giambono is the only Venetian here who antedates the art-movement which had Padua for its seat and Squarcione for its figure-head. The part Squarcione himself played in the actual making of the young artists was probably no greater than that played by

[1] I feel certain now that this is by Giambono.

[2] Other works that I have every reason to believe to be by Giambono are a "St. Nicholas of Bari," and a "St. Augustine," in the Sacristy of the Salute, and Nos. 26 and 28 in Sala VII. of the Museo Correr, in Venice.

M. Julian in the Parisian *ateliers* of to-day. It is more than probable that Squarcione, like M. Julian at present, did no more than afford students an opportunity of working together and profiting by the presence, if not the actual instruction, of the great artists employed in the same town. In Padua masters such as Jacopo Bellini, Donatello, and Fra Filippo were all at work, and the younger men certainly studied their productions, and, it may be, enjoyed their actual teaching. It still remains for some investigator to reconstruct this art-movement, showing just what influences and what personalities went to form it, and I venture to prophesy that the result of such researches will be to prove that, deducting the Florentine elements, the so-called School of Squarcione was nothing but an embryonic phase of the Venetian school.[1]

To the man of supreme genius who all his life long remained most faithful to the Squarcionesque traditions, to ANDREA MANTEGNA, no less than nine separate works in this exhibition are attributed. Of these, two only are his without question, No. 22, the "Adoration of the Magi," belonging to Louisa, Lady Ashburton, and No. 96, a "Holy Family," belonging to Mr. Ludwig Mond. The "Adoration" is not treated here in the usual Epiphany spirit, but severely and hieratically. Besides the Child, there are only five other figures. Crowded as a composition and rather gaudy in colour, with its bright reds and yellows and streaks of chocolate dye, the picture could never have been a source of great delight to a cultivated eye, and the disfiguring varnish which now covers the greater

---

[1] Squarcione himself now seems to me to have been a painter of some merit. His one authentic picture, the "Madonna" at Berlin (No. 27A), was painted by a man who, in a way, was a real master.

part of it, makes it even more difficult to do the work justice. Considered for its quality of line, however, it is admirable, and as feeling it has much of that tender homeliness which characterized Mantegna at a certain time, as appears in the Poldi-Pezzoli, the Bergamo, and the Dresden " Madonnas," and in the Berlin " Circumcision." The " Adoration " slightly antedates most of the pictures just mentioned, and shows every affinity in morphology and technique with the Hampton Court cartoons, the earliest of which must have been produced at exactly the same time. As a composition on a theme so hackneyed, it seems to have struck Mantegna's fellow craftsmen for its originality, for we find numerous versions of it by nondescript painters in many of the Italian provincial galleries. The movement of the Madonna and Child seems particularly to have attracted attention. Bonsignori copied it in an interesting "Madonna" belonging to Dr. J. P. Richter, and an inferior imitation of it is actually hanging on the same wall, No. 12, a " Virgin, Child and Donor," attributed to Previtali, but really, as we shall see later, by another Bergamask painter, Francesco Santa Croce.

Not very dissimilar in technique, although probably a trifle earlier in date, and of a quality incomparably superior, is Mr. Mond's " Holy Family " (No. 96). The Christ Child, half draped in white, with the look and carriage of an infant emperor, stands on the top of an elliptical wall, looking like the rim of a well, but representing, the catalogue tells us, the " Hortus Clausus." Beside him stands the infant John, pointing to him with an appealing look. On a level with them, to the R., appears the noble head of St. Joseph, and within the " Hortus Clausus " we see in profile the bust of the Virgin bending forward in prayer. These figures, outlined with gem-like precision, and of the most refined severity of expression, are relieved against a dark orange-tree on which glistens the golden fruit. Whether we consider this canvas from the point of view of line, or of colour—a quality of which Mantegna is not often absolute master— whether from the point of view of modelling or of expression, we shall rarely find its rival among the other works of the great Paduan, and never its superior.

Lord Pembroke's "Judith" (No. 125) is a small panel which, although I am persuaded it is not by Mantegna himself, is not to be dismissed lightly. The composition differs considerably from both the well-known versions of this subject by Mantegna, from the cameo-like drawing in the Uffizi, so antique in form and so modern in feeling, and from the superb mono-chrome recently belonging to Col. Malcolm.[1] Lord Pembroke's tiny panel recalls rather Zuan Andrea's engraving, and there are faults in it which Mantegna himself would scarcely have made. The head of the Judith, although grandly antique, is extremely hard in modelling, and the old attendant, in her effort to preserve her balance while she holds open the mouth of the bag which is to receive Holofernes' head, as-sumes an attitude which is almost ludicrous. The colouring is gaudy yellow and pink in proportions un-known to me in any of Mantegna's genuine works, and in the drawing, despite the correctness, there is an element of pettiness which, I think, betrays rather than the obedient hand of the creator, the painful effort of the strenuous imitator. And besides all these objections to this little "Judith," comes one which perhaps outweighs them all. It is this: in the work of a master whose evolution may be pursued from first to last with scarcely a break, any given genuine

[1] Now in the National Gallery at Dublin.

picture must have its easily determinable place, if not actually between two well accredited pictures, at least in a small group of determined date. Now, few artists have had a more steady evolution than Mantegna. Every picture offering itself as a work of his must therefore be able to marshal itself in line with its unquestioned compeers before we may accept it. But Lord Pembroke's "Judith" will hunt in vain for such companions. Certainly it will not find its natural place beside the Uffizi Triptych, from which it differs in form and in colour, as well as in quality; and even less will it take rank among works which share much of its own hardness, the now scattered San Zeno *predelle* (in the Louvre and at Tours), or the "Agony in the Garden" recently acquired from Lord Northbrook by the National Gallery. From all of these it is widely divergent in spirit no less than in colour. The closest kin of this "Judith" is really such a picture as the small "St. Sebastian" of Vienna (Imperial Gallery, No. 81), in which also, in spite of the Greek signature, and in spite of its many merits, I have never been able to see the touch of Mantegna himself. I see in them both achievements of remarkably competent imitators, if indeed they are not both by the same hand.[1]

Less able, though still excellent imitations after Mantegna, are two small monochrome canvases belonging to Mr. R. A. Markham,[2] the one representing "Dido," and the other "Judith" once more (Nos. 21 and 24). They are pendants executed by the same

[1] No, they are not by the same hand. The "Sebastian" now seems to me a genuine work of Mantegna's earliest Mantuan period. The Pembroke "Judith" I find more puzzling than ever. If by Mantegna himself, it can scarcely have been painted much before 1490. But how account for the stiff, miniature-like precision, at this late date?

[2] Now to Mr. J. E. Tayler.

clever hand that produced the "Summer" and "Autumn" of the National Gallery (No. 1125), there attributed to Mantegna himself. Between all such imitations and the genuine works there is a difference, easily overlooked, it is true, but of mortal consequence—the difference in quality.

We need not be detained by Mr. J. B. Carrington's "Entombment" (No. 71), an obviously modern coloured copy after an engraving; nor by Nos. 308 and 309, drawings from the Queen's collection, attributed on very slight provocation to Mantegna himself. We cannot, however, so lightly pass by Mr. Charles Butler's "Madonna" (No. 4). It is catalogued as a replica of a picture at Berlin (No. 27), which passed, until recently, for an unquestioned Mantegna, but which has in the last catalogue been conceded as the work of assistants, or possibly of "the young Giovanni Bellini, under the influence of Mantegna and Donatello." As Mr. Butler's picture, allowing for its worse preservation, is identical with the one in Berlin, so far as the Madonna and Child are concerned, I will discuss the two works together. The differences are that the landscape background here is replaced by a plain blue background in the Berlin picture, while the crowned head of Paduan character on the parapet here is there changed to an empty *cartellino*. The Berlin "Madonna," moreover, is framed in by a border containing naked little angels holding the instruments of the Passion, with bronzed cherubs separating the groups. Let us now analyze these pictures. The Madonnas in type, dress, and expression resemble no universally acknowledged work by Mantegna, but closely approach Bartolommeo Vivarini's signed "Madonna" in the National Gallery (No. 284). The drawing of the eyes, the nose, the mouth, and the hands is equally Vivarinesque, but—Bartolommeo never models so plastically and so classically. In this point the works are Mantegnesque ; and even more Mantegnesque is the Child, whose ear, and whose close folds of linen drapery have everything of Mantegna except the quality. Coming to the border of the Berlin picture, we are struck at once by the little nudes executed with anything but charm, and betraying an altogether different conception of the naked *putto* from B. Vivarini's. The cherubs, on the other hand, recall the latter (cf. Naples altar-piece) far more than Mantegna. There is nothing whatever of Giovanni Bellini in these works, but, as our analysis tells us, we here have to deal with a person who stands between B. Vivarini and Mantegna. We should be forced to refuse the hypothesis of Mantegna by the crudeness of the cherubs, the heaviness of the *putti*, and the lifelessness of the line throughout, even if there were not so much to remind us of Vivarini ; while for the latter, even setting aside the many Mantegnesque motives, the work is too classical and too plastic. Its real author must have been a person trained to the habits of Bartolommeo Vivarini, and incapable of shaking them off even when making every effort to imitate Mantegna. Just who he was, what name he had, is a problem still to be determined. Judging from the dates of those works of Mantegna and of B. Vivarini that these " Madonnas " most resemble—the Mantegnas in the Uffizi, and the National Gallery Vivarini, along with his signed works at Venice and Naples of 1464 and 1465—these two pictures must have been painted between 1460 and 1470.

　　　　　　　　　　　　　　　　　　　　　　　　[Panciatichi-Ximenes Collection, Florence

A PIETÀ

III.

To BARTOLOMMEO VIVARINI two works are attributed, both school pictures, however. Mr. G.
McNeil Rushforth's "Madonna" (No. 33) seems
originally to have had a gold background which it
pleased some later possessor to cover with a landscape. Mr. Charles Butler's "Death of the Virgin"
(No. 44) is interesting as showing the way the subject was treated by the Muranese painters; otherwise it is of little value. The inscription, OPVS
FACTVM VENETIIS PER BARTHOLOMEVM VIVARINVM DE
MVRIANO, 1480, is, as has been pointed out, and as is
indeed obvious, a plain statement of the fact that it
is a work done at the orders or under the super-
vision of Bartolommeo, but not by himself, and for
a non-Venetian destination, the word *Venetiis* being
of consequence only to provincial owners.

IV.

Nowhere else in the world can CARLO CRIVELLI,
Bartolommeo Vivarini's exact contemporary and
fellow-pupil under Antonio da Murano and "Squarcione," be studied as in London, where at least nineteen of his works are known to me. Eight of these,
among the most splendid, are in the National
Gallery; the remainder exist in private collections,
and, of these, eight are now exhibited in the New
Gallery. It is a pity that the earliest of all the
English Crivellis is not on exhibition—I mean the
highly interesting "Madonna" belonging to Sir

Francis Cook, which in type and characteristics is more advanced than the polyptych at Massa Fermana, dated 1468 (reproduced, as are the bulk of Crivelli's works, in Mr. Rushforth's scholarly book on this painter, London, Bell), and not so mature as the lovely "Madonna," dated 1470, in the library at Macerata, and which may therefore safely be dated 1469. The earliest, as well as the most dainty and charming, among the exhibited pictures is the small pale-coloured "Madonna" of supreme refinement, which belongs to Lord Northbrook (No. 42), signed OPVS KAROLI CRIVELLI VENETI). In character and quality it stands very close to the Macerata picture. Of about the same date is the "Resurrection" (No. 50) from the same collection. Scarcely, if at all, later than these is a work in which Crivelli in his quality of design, in the enamel of his surface, and in the energy of his line, approaches closer than any other Occidental artist to what is the supreme quality of Japanese art, particularly as manifested in lacquer. Besides all this charm as pattern, the "St. George and the Dragon"—the work to which I allude (No. 40, formerly in the Leyland collection, and now the property of Mr. Stuart M. Samuel[1])— has that feeling of the fairy-tale about it which makes it imperative that it should have, as it has here, a sky of gold. In this respect it recalls another version of the same subject, by some as yet unidentified early Venetian, the one in the Martinengo Gallery at Brescia, there ascribed to Montorfano.[2] Mrs. Robert Benson's "Madonna" (No. 32, inscribed CAROLVS CRIVELLVS VENETVS PINSIT, 1472), not quite so enchanting as the preceding works, is nevertheless full of charm, and, in point of date, follows close

[1] Now belonging to Mrs. J. L. Gardner, of Boston, U.S.A.
[2] Possibly the author of this was Quirico da Murano.

QUIRICO DA MURANO (?)

ST. GEORGE AND THE DRAGON

Alinari Photo.

[*Martinengo Gallery, Brescia.*]

upon them. The virgin's facing to the left, and the child's eager movement to the right indicate that this panel must have formed originally the middle of a polyptych, with saints on either side. Of later date and minor interest are the "St. George" and the "St. Dominic" (Nos. 86 and 88) belonging to Louisa, Lady Ashburton, and Lord Northbrook's "St. Catherine and St. Bernardino" (No. 302). The exhibition is, furthermore, fortunate in having a superb specimen of a theme treated by Crivelli frequently and always with the greatest passion and mastery—the "Pietà." Mr. R. Crawshay's "Pietà" (No. 87, formerly in the Dudley collection) has not, perhaps, quite the concentration, either in grouping or feeling, of the one in the Panciatichi collection at Florence, dated 1485, but it stands very close to it in quality as well as in date.

Two further works in the New Gallery are ascribed to Carlo Crivelli (No. 5), a "Triptych," belonging to Mr. S. Milner Gibson Cullum, and No. 48, a "Madonna," belonging to Sir William Farrer. In the "Triptych," the hand of Vittorio Crivelli will at once be recognized by anybody who happens to be acquainted with the signed or otherwise authenticated works by this follower of Carlo, with which the region between Fermo, Ascoli, and Sarnano, in the March of Ancona, is teeming. The "Madonna" is by an even inferior person, Pietro Alamanno, who, like the Crivelli, a native of Venice,[1] worked a great deal at Ascoli, where a number of his feeble imitations of the great Crivelli are still preserved.

[1] This is proved by a "Polyptych" by him, in part, which belongs to Mr. Foulke, of Paris. Alamanno's panel, the central one, bears the signature, PETRVS VENETVS PINSIT—thus proving that he was not, as Messrs. Crowe and Cavalcaselle supposed, a native of Ascoli.

V.

Once passed through its Squarcionesque phase, Venetian painting runs on smoothly to its apogee in Giorgione and Titian, headed meanwhile by three great masters, ALVISE VIVARINI, Gentile Bellini, and Giovanni Bellini, each of whom stands for a distinct tendency, each of whom has a following of his own. They emerge together from the Paduan vortex, and although their common origin is apparent to the end, they travel further and further apart, Alvise devoting himself chiefly to the expression of very intensely felt spiritual emotion, and to striking portraiture; Gentile to historical and ceremonial painting; and Giovanni Bellini to the exploitation of the dawning sense of beauty, to the perception of which in the life about them the study of the recovered ancient art was leading the best minds. In threading our way through the remainder of the pictures exhibited in the New Gallery, we shall do best to discuss separately the works of each of the schools mentioned, beginning with that of ALVISE, which to the end carried along with it a greater residuum of the old traditions than either of the other schools. I shall, I trust, be pardoned for proceeding on the assumption that the reconstruction of Alvise Vivarini and his school, given in my book on Lorenzo Lotto,[1] is, in its main features, correct. On this hypothesis, Cima da Conegliano, Montagna, Basaiti, and Andrea Solario—to mention only artists represented in this collection—formed an integral part of the school of

[1] "Lorenzo Lotto, an essay in Constructive Art Criticism." G. P. Putnam's Sons, London and New York, 1895.

PORTRAIT OF A YOUTH

Alvise, while Antonello da Messina was closely connected with it.

To Alvise himself a work is attributed, which, if it were really his, would go far to justify the neglect into which he has fallen. It is a *predella* in three parts, representing the " Death of the Virgin " (No. 6, belonging to Mrs. B. W. Currie). It is of a style and of a period when the Venetian school was not yet quite differentiated from the other North Italian schools which passed through the Squarcionesque mould. At first sight, therefore, these panels tempt one to think of some Ferrarese master—some crude brother of Ercole Roberti. Further examination reveals, however, certain mannerisms and something of the spirit—if such a word may be used in connection with so stupid a person!—of Lazzaro Sebastiani, who, in his earlier years, was a close follower of the Vivarini, and at the end of the fifteenth century became the abject imitator of Gentile Bellini and Carpaccio.

Fortunately there is a real Alvise in this exhibition, and a work to do his fame no discredit ; but it passes, as a number of his portraits do, under the name of Antonello da Messina (No. 142, belonging to Mr. George Salting [1]). It is the portrait of a boy of fifteen or sixteen, a little defiant and shy, yet frank in look, with a *zazzara* of blonde hair cropped short over the eyebrows, wearing a coat of pale turquoise with a dark band across it. To give all my reasons for assigning this portrait to Alvise would mean repeating the demonstration given in my " Lotto." Here it must suffice to draw attention to the colouring, the outline of the face, the precise look of the eyes, and the precise arrangement of the hair, in all of which points it is divergent from Antonello, and

[1] Exhibited on loan at the National Gallery.

like the portraits, particularly such an one as Lady
Layard's at Venice, which I have ascribed to Alvise,
I trust on sufficient grounds. This little bust of Mr.
Salting's is the only Alvise here, but not the only
one in or near London. Another belongs to Sir
Charles Robinson,[1] who attributes it also to Antonello, and another still is at Windsor Castle, where
it passes under the name of Leonardo. They are
both among the greatest achievements which Venetian art attained before the triumph of the Giorgionesque.[2]

VI.

I am, happily, not the first to question the pro-
priety of attributing Mr. Salting's portrait to Antonello. Messrs. Crowe and Cavalcaselle have also
rejected this attribution. Instead, they would assign
this boy's head to ANDREA SOLARIO. Little as I can
agree with them, their idea is not so far-fetched as
it may seem. Solario, in his earlier phase, was more
of a Venetian than a Lombard painter.[3] The few
years he passed in Venice, during the last decade of
the fifteenth century, left an indelible impression
upon him. He seems, at that time, to have been
greatly exposed to the influence of Alvise Vivarini ;
and, although it is scarcely likely that he was personally acquainted with Antonello, he appears to

[1] Now to the Countess de Béarn of Paris.
[2] No. 236, the "Bust of a Man," with long hair and brown
beard, is a feeble work of Alvisesque character. It is unascribed,
and belongs to Mr. Henry Willett.
[3] Cf. "Lorenzo Lotto," p. 119, note.

have been strongly attracted by such of his works as could then be seen in Venice. Of this we have a singular proof in a panel now exhibited in the New Gallery under the name of Antonello himself (No. 131, belonging to Sir Francis Cook), but really by no other than Solario. It is a bust of Christ, crowned with thorns, and tied to a column, with mouth open and eyes turned upwards—a fairly exact copy of the Antonello in the Venice Academy (No. 589, photographed by Anderson, No. 11536). At first sight, one can scarcely think of anyone but Antonello ; and the suggestion of the true authorship of this picture will probably give others as much of a shock as it did me, when it was first made to me by Signor Gustavo Frizzoni, the most competent living judge of Lombard art. But detailed inspection soon reveals the justice of its attribution to Solario. The execution, far from being, as we find it in the Venice panel, of a brutality to equal the conception, is rather dainty—almost refined. The glazes are far more transparent than those of Antonello, and the colouring very much paler. In technique and colour the panel before us is, in fact, absolutely identical with Solario's signed " Madonna and Saints," in the Brera (No. 106), which was painted at Murano in 1495 : and also with another early " Madonna," belonging to Signor Crespi, of Milan. Sir Francis Cook's picture has, in common with these " Madonnas," the almost white, porcelain-like flesh painting ; and closely resembles another well-known Solario, the " Ecce Homo " of the Poldi Pezzoli Museum, in the pearl-like tears rolling down the cheek of Christ—painted in a way so peculiar to Solario. An open-minded person, who could see all these pictures juxtaposed, would not hesitate to acknowledge the same hand in the " Christ at the Column" as in the other three undisputed Solarios.[1]

VII.

To CIMA DA CONEGLIANO, Alvise's closest and, barring Lotto, ablest follower, ten separate works are here attributed. Of these, three only can be counted genuine—Lord Browlow's unexpected and exquisite little "Santa Conversazione" (No. 53), and Mr. Mond's recent acquisitions from the Eastlake sale, a "St. Mark" (No. 239), and a "St. Sebastian" (No. 245). Of the remainder, Mr. L. Lesser's "Madonna" (No. 28) is too painful an object, and of too recent a date, for us to linger over, while Mr. Charles Butler's "Ecce Homo" (No. 102) is nothing but a copy of a picture by Cima in the National Gallery (No. 1310), there ascribed to Giovanni Bellini. Mr. Salting's "Virgin" (No. 113) is a Cimaesque work by the desolatingly prolific and almost incredibly protean Girolamo Santacroce.[2] Sir Francis Cook's "Head of Christ" (No.

[1] To Antonello, who really is not represented at all in this exhibition, three other works are attributed. The "Veronica" (No. 10, belonging to Mr. G. Donaldson) is a weak thing of Antonello-Alvisesque character, possibly by Filippo Mazzola. The "Portrait of Hans Memling" (No. 59) is a poor copy of the Antonello portrait in the National Gallery. The drawing for an "Adoration of the Magi" (No. 329) is not worth notice.

[2] Were Girolamo Santacroce now living, he would undoubtedly be a chromo-lithographer, supplying popular devotion with the chromos of sacred subjects to be found in chapels, and in the houses of the lower classes in Catholic countries. Other paintings by him in this exhibition are a "Resurrection" (No. 55), lent by the Corporation of Liverpool; a "Riposo" (No. 122) in his later manner, belonging to Captain Holford; a "Madonna and Saints" (No. 7), belonging to the same owner, and ascribed to Titian; and, finally, a "Madonna and Saints" pilfered from Bissolo (No. 60), attributed to Previtali (lent by Lord Northbrook). The "Madonna and Saints" (No. 139), which is exhibited by Mr. Charles Butler, as Girolamo, is too poor even for him.

HOLY FAMILY IN A LANDSCAPE

135) is a puzzling picture. The features strangely recall those of the young Dürer, the mannerisms suggest Barbari, the colouring makes one think of Cima, while a certain mincingness and coldness seem to indicate a Flemish hand. Possibly we have here a work by some Flemish master, painted at Venice in the last years of the fifteenth century. As to Mr. Charles Butler's "Saviour" (No. 23), Sir B. Samuelson's "Madonna and Saints" (No. 143), and Sir M. S. Stewart's "Madonna" (No. 146), they are probably, as we shall see, by Rocco Marconi, Rondinelli, and Basaiti respectively.

Returning now to the real Cimas, there is little to be said about Mr. Mond's panels, except that they are excellent average specimens of Cima's art. Lord Brownlow's "Santa Conversazione" is conceived like a large altar-piece, but is executed in miniature, and, while retaining breadth of execution, is treated with gem-like precision. It is a fascinating composition. I can do no better than quote the description given in the catalogue : " Small full-length figures in a landscape with buildings in the background ; in the centre, the Virgin seated under a tree with the Child on her knee, who turns towards an angel in attitude of adoration ; behind them, St. Joseph ; and on the right St. Catherine ; on the left another angel, her hands crossed on her breast, and St. John the Baptist."

To this I would add that the Madonna and the rock platform on which she sits are almost the same as in the Vienna altar-piece (No. 19) ; that the landscape has Cima's best effects of mist hovering at the foot of the distant mountains ; and that the work to which this little jewel stands closest is the Dresden " Presentation of the Virgin " (No. 63). Besides these, there is exhibited a drawing from the Windsor collection (No. 307) which represents a Bishop enthroned in a chapel with Saints on either side of him. This drawing is probably by Cima, and of great value, as it is nearly if not absolutely unique.

VIII.

The only painter who has, thus far, been recognized as a follower of Alvise Vivarini is MARCO BASAITI. He was by no means the worst of Alvise's following, but a mediocrity all the same. He holds about the same relation to Alvise and his greater pupils that Lorenzo di Credi holds to Verocchio and Leonardo ; indeed, the parallel between them is so exact that Basaiti may well be called the Credi of Venetian art. Both these painters lacked not only the force to strike out for themselves, but even the wit to acquire what their masters could teach them. Only three pictures are attributed to Basaiti in this exhibition, and of these one (the "St. Jerome," No. 62, lent by the Corporation of Liverpool) is nothing but a poor copy of a Montagna belonging to Signor Gustavo Frizzoni of Milan. The other two are genuine, Mrs. Benson's "Bust of a Noble" (No. 25, signed M. BASA) being a ruined work of his last years, and Mr. Salting's "Madonna" (No, 101, signed MARCO BASAITI, P.) being a very early work of little artistic quality, wherein all the Alvisesque mannerisms are exaggerated. But there are at least two, and possibly three other and more important works by Basaiti in this collection, all belonging to Mrs. Robert Benson, and all attributed to Giovanni Bellini, two of them actually bearing the supposed signature of this great master.

The most important of these is a large rectangular

BASAITI

VIRGIN AND CHILD WITH FOUR SAINTS

picture (No. 107), thirty-eight inches high by sixty wide.   Until Morelli cast his eyes upon it, it passed as an unquestioned masterpiece by Giovanni Bellini. To Morelli it was, and to most of his following it remains, "the triumph of Bissolo's art."   My intention here is not to demonstrate that this picture is not by Giovanni Bellini (I take it for granted that this will scarcely be questioned), but to prove that Bissolo had nothing to do with it, and that its real author was Basaiti.   To begin with, let us glance at the composition.   The Saints are arranged on either side of the Madonna in separate tiers, a form of grouping always affected by Alvise and frequently by his followers, but never by Bellini and his close followers, least of all by Bissolo.   But the composition is by no means the only Alvisesque trait in this work.   The Madonna, although she distantly recalls the type found in Bellini's Madonnas at St.   Francesco della Vigna at Venice, and in the Brera (No. 297), recalls much more strongly Basaiti's National Gallery Madonna (No. 599), while the bend of her head and her kerchief, as well as the position and movement of the Child, vividly call up the Alvise " Madonna" belonging to M. Loeser, of Florence, now (not exhibited) in the National Gallery.   The St. John, although he may have something that suggests the Baptist in Bellini's picture at Santa Corona in Vicenza, yet has the Alvisesque peculiarity—never occurring in Bellini—of the pointing forefinger.   The St. Catherine is not only a mere variation upon Alvise's " St. Giustina" in the Bagati collection at Milan, but partakes of most of the characteristics of Alvise's early picture in the Venice Academy, the " St. Lawrence."   I would also call attention to the striking likeness, not only in face but in form of hand, between this St. Catherine and Lotto's in the altar-piece by the latter in St. Bartolommeo at Bergamo.[1] Finally, the St. Peter is a type found in Basaiti's "Madonna with SS. Peter and Liberale" in the Museum of Padua, and his hand with the long thumb drawn as far away as possible from the fingers, is the typical Alvisesque hand. Now all these Alvisesque traits and all these likenesses to Basaiti point unmistakably to this painter, and not to Bissolo, who is strictly Bellinesque, with different forms and different sentiment.

I have lingered so long over this picture because of its importance in itself, and as a factor in determining our estimate of the painter to whom we ascribe it. In so far as it recalls Bellini at all, it recalls pictures painted, as we know, about 1510, and thus leads us to infer that it was executed at about this date. Possibly Basaiti was then employed by Bellini, who, after the death of Alvise (in 1503), and of Gentile (in 1507), remained the one great master to whom people in Venice, or under Venetian influence, would naturally turn for their pictures. How far he was from being able to supply the demand we know from the difficulty experienced by so high a patroness as Isabella d'Este, in getting from him something for herself. He seems to have been too busy to furnish even cartoons, and therefore to have allowed his abler assistants to paint what they liked, for him to sell as coming from his factory, and bearing his trade-mark. This *may* be the explanation of the signature on Mrs. Benson's altar-piece, which is in script—no universally accepted Bellini is thus signed—although the coarseness of its execution gives me some doubt of its authenticity.[2]

---

[1] She should be compared with still another figure by an Alvisesque painter, with Bonsignori's Female Saint in the Poldi Museum, there ascribed to Costa.

[2] A very recent theory of German art-criticism would ascribe

If this hypothesis of Basaiti's relation to Bellini
be correct, it would perfectly account for the other
of Mrs. Benson's Basaitis, which is signed Bellini,
with a signature apparently old. This is a little
"St. Jerome" (No. 169) of very Alvisesque character, with locks of hair exactly paralleled in the work
of two of Alvise's other pupils, Cima and Jacopo di
Barbari,[1] with an Alvisesque hand, sitting in front
of a landscape which recalls several of Basaiti's, particularly the one in the Venetian version of the
"Calling of Zebedee's Children" (Venice Academy,
No. 39). The rocks are horn-coloured, as we find
them constantly in Basaiti and never in Bellini, and
the deep blue sky resembles a very Alvisesque work
hanging close by, "Lotto's "Danaë" (No. 80, belonging to Mr. Conway). If the date, 1505, be
genuine, as is probable, then it proves that Basaiti
lost little time in finding steady employment with
Bellini, once having finished the altar-piece in the
Frari left unfinished by Alvise upon his death in
1503.

The third of Mrs. Benson's Bellinis that I believe
to be by Basaiti is the little "Infant Bacchus" (No.
167). I am led to this conclusion by the sharp
blues, and the forms and tone of the landscape. At
all events, even if by Basaiti, it is only a copy of a
picture belonging to Mr. Mond (formerly in the
Habich collection), the conception and execution
of which are both so thoroughly in the manner of
Carotto that it is impossible not to believe that this
Veronese artist must have originated the composition, as well as painted it.[2]

this and certain other works that I have given to Basaiti to—
"Pseudo-Basaiti."
[1] To Barbari a non-Italian portrait (No. 117) is falsely attributed.
[2] When I wrote thus I was unacquainted with the famous Bac-

IX.

An interesting and powerful painter, whom, in my recent book on Lotto I have tried to bring into connection with Alvise, is BARTOLOMMEO MONTAGNA, an artist who happens to be remarkably well represented in this gallery. Seven pictures are attributed to him, and two drawings, and of these, four of the paintings and one of the drawings actually are by him, while his also are two charming little *tondi* ascribed to Carpaccio. Of all these pictures the first in date is Sir William Farrer's " Madonna " (No. 72), perhaps the freshest and most charming, as well as the earliest of all Montagna's existing works. The composition is the not infrequent Alvisesque one of the Virgin bending slightly over the Child whom she holds in her arms—a composition such as we have already seen in Mrs. Benson's large Basaiti. In the Montagna, as in that picture, and in most Alvisesque works, the Child is thin-haired, large-headed, and chubby-limbed. His ear has the nick into the cheek so rarely absent from the works of Alvise's followers. The Madonna's pupils are rolled a trifle too low, a fault not infrequent among the Vivarini, as in the Child in Alvise's " Madonna " of 1480, in the Venice Academy (No.

chanal painted in 1514 in Giambellino's workshop, in great part, I believe, by Basaiti. In one corner of that composition we find an infant Bacchus, who doubtless was the prototype of Mrs. Benson's picture. Carotto therefore was the copyist, and not Basaiti.

Sir M. S. Stewart's " Madonna " (No. 146), attributed, as we have already noticed, to Cima, seems to be, in so far as the present condition of the panel permits of a judgment, also by Basaiti.

B. MONTAGNA

[*Sir William Farrer*

MADONNA AND CHILD

607), in Bartolommeo's "Magdalen," in the same collection (No. 584), and in the "Madonna," from Alvise's *atelier* at Piove del Sacco, near Padua. The landscape, with its jagged peaks, cliffs, and little trees, remains within the Vivarinesque canon, reminding us of Alvise's own landscapes, of the landscapes of Basaiti, in Mr. Salting's "Madonna" already mentioned, of Lazzaro Sebastiani's landscape in his "Nativity" of the Venice Academy (No. 100), and even of the landscapes of Crivelli. Another Alvisesque trick that I must not forget to mention —Alvisesque, although afterwards so much exploited by Giorgione and his following—is the exposure of the last joints only of the fingers, as in the Madonna's right hand here. A little later, maturer, but, perhaps, somewhat less fresh, and certainly less gay in colour, is the "Madonna" belonging to Miss Hertz (No. 78)—one of the masterpieces of Venetian art, nevertheless. It is already so well known that I need not linger over it here. Suffice it to say that, morphologically as well as qualitatively, it stands the most searching criticism, in spite of the fact that the Madonna is of a type which was adopted, with the soul gone out of it and the features caricatured, by the clod-hopping Marcello Fogolino. Of a later and nearly identical period of Montagna's career are the "Madonnas" belonging to Lord Cowper (No. 17, signed OPVS BARTHOLOMEI M.), and to Sir B. Samuelson (No. 69), both of rich, bituminous colouring, with dark landscapes. The *tondi*, originally from a wedding *cassone*, belong, like the first "Madonna," to Sir William Farrer, who thus possesses examples of Montagna's latest as well as earliest style. They represent the "Story of Claudia" (No. 132) and a "Marriage Scene" (No. 134), and although they pass under the name of

Carpaccio, the heroic types, the large and angular draperies, and the powerful brick reds, leave no doubt whatever as to their real authorship, especially as we have their exact mates in a well-known work by Montagna, the two *tondi* still remaining on the original *cassone* in the Museo Poldi-Pezzoli at Milan (photographed by Marcozzi).

Of the drawings, the " Head of the Virgin " from the Windsor collection (No. 310, in charcoal) is, it is true, authentic, although it is not, as stated in the catalogue, a study for the picture in the Brera. Of the other works attributed to Montagna, the drawing of a " Male Figure holding a Globe " (No. 311), is by nobody in particular ; Mrs. Horner's little " St. Gabriel " (No. 38), rejuvenated though it has been, clearly betrays both in the draperies and in the sky, the hand of Michele da Verona ; and the Duke of Norfolk's two organ shutters with "St. Bartholomew " on the one (No. 36) and " St. Augustine " on the other (No. 45), are Montagnesque indeed, but feeble in drawing and of an entirely different scheme of colour from his. Although Montagna may have supervised the execution of these figures (originally in San Bartolommeo at Vicenza), the hand that I recognize in them is that of one of his pupils, interesting not only on his own account but for the race of artists whom he begat, I mean the elder Francesco da Ponte, surnamed Bassano, with whose authenticated works, now preserved in the gallery of his native town, these organ shutters have striking points of resemblance.

In this connection, I must speak of those of Montagna's other pupils who happen to be represented in the New Gallery. Although Giovanni Buonconsiglio, surnamed *Mareschalco*, is not once mentioned in the catalogue, he was the author of at least two

and probably four, pictures in this exhibition. One
of them is even signed. It is an " Ecce Homo "
(No. 54, belonging to Mr. T. Humphry Ward), of a
very Montagnesque character, a variation on his
master's treatment of the subject in the Louvre (No.
1393), but melodramatic as is the character of Buonconsiglio, although not so passionate as his later
" Ecce Homo " in Lady Layard's collection at Venice.
Clearly though the colour and treatment and spirit
of Mr. Ward's picture prove it to be by Buonconsiglio, it is yet ascribed to Speranza, because the
latter also was called Giovanni, and the signature is
IOANNES VICENTINVS PINSIT. Now not only is Speranza's style different from and inferior to this, but he
is not so likely to have signed "VICENTINVS" as
Buonconsiglio, who in the flower of his years worked
away from home in Venice, where he would have
been sufficiently designated, as Speranza living in
Vicenza would not, by the name "John of Vicenza."
A later work by the same master is the very poor
" Holy Family with the Infant John and two other
Saints" also belonging to Mr. Ward (No. 14). In
this picture we have a hasty work of Buonconsiglio's
declining art, but yet a work which in types and
forms recalls his grand altar-piece of 1502 in San
Rocco at Vicenza. As Mareschalco was still living
in 1530, it is natural that in his later years he should
have attempted to adopt the vogue of Giorgionesque
subjects and treatment. In this light we see him in
an almost charming open-air " Concert " in the
Vicenza Gallery (Sala III., No. 94), in a " Resurrection " in the Carrara Gallery at Bergamo, and in an
" Agony in the Garden " in the Rovigo Gallery
(No. 127, ascribed to Mantegna). It is in this on
the whole painful phase of Buonconsiglio's career,
when as an old man, and always rather uncouth, he

was trying to imitate the mere trappings of the everlasting youthfulness of Giorgione, that we see him, if I mistake not, in Captain Holford's " Lady with a Man in Armour" (No. 75) (the colour, cut of mouth, and look betray Mareschalco), and in Mr. Charles Butler's " Mistress of Giorgione" (No. 275, attributed to Giorgione himself). Speranza, whom I have already mentioned, an impotent imitator of Montagna, is the author of a very small " Holy Family" (No. 81), belonging to M. Léon Somzée, which has all the characteristics of niggling outline and chromo-like colouring of his signed pictures in the Brera and at Vicenza.

X.

Putting aside for the moment Catena, who, although he began with Alvise, yet did most of his work under the influence of the Bellini, Carpaccio and Giorgione, we have now examined all the Alvisesque pictures in this exhibition, and are ready to turn to the paintings of the Bellineschi, first to those of Gentile and his following, and then to those of Giovanni and his.[1]

To GENTILE four different works are attributed. Of these, the two slight portraits lent by the Oxford University Galleries (Nos. 39 and 43) are nondescript works of the Veronese school, while the black chalk drawing of " Two Portraits of Men" (No. 325,

[1] There is no genuine work by Jacopo Bellini in this exhibition. "The Dominican Preaching" (No. 3, lent by the Oxford University Galleries,) is of the school of Domenico Morone of Verona. The church represented is, by the way, Sant' Eufemia of that town.

Dixon Photo.]   [*Mr. Ludwig Mond.*

MADONNA AND CHILD

lent by Sir C. Robinson) is nothing at all. The fourth, however—Mr. Ludwig Mond's " Virgin and Child " (No. 47, signed OPVS GENTILIS BELLINI VENETI, EQVITIS)—is a well-known genuine work, which was until recently in the Eastlake collection. In its present condition, this picture is more interesting than delightful, and it must always have been spoiled by the uncouth throne, in the worst Italian taste, upon which the Virgin is seated. Nor was this the subject to be well treated by Gentile. Although (as the title in the signature indicates) he must have painted this picture at the beginning of the eighties, at a time when Giovanni was already portraying his most unconventional and touching Madonnas, Gentile's Virgin is hieratic, almost Byzantine, and betrays no advance upon the model left him by his father Jacopo, vividly recalling, in fact, a Virgin by the latter which is now in the Tadini Gallery at Lovere (Photographed by Oliari of Brescia).

It is not to paintings like this that we must turn if we wish to form an adequate conception of this, perhaps greatest of pre-Giorgionesque Venetians, but to his few portraits and to his historical paintings, which are, unfortunately, even rarer—most of his works having been destroyed by fire and other accidents. Considering the scarcity of this great master, we the more eagerly study his faithful follower and vulgariser, VITTORE CARPACCIO.

XI.

We do not see him here in his most characteristic capacity, that of a *raconteur*, but as the author of one figure of a saint, and of a couple of drawings. The saint is a charming representation of a woman, dressed in the gay costume of the time, seated by a lake side, reading (No. 49, lent by Mrs. Robert Benson), perhaps, the fragment of some "Santa Conversazione."[1] The drawings are—one from the Windsor collection (No. 306, pen and bistre, washed), representing the "Presentation of the Virgin," and containing a fanciful version of Bramante's St. Peter's in the background; while the other is a fine sketch for a "Portrait of a Bearded Man," which is lent by Sir C. Robinson (No. 341, black chalk and bistre, heightened with white).

The catalogue, however, attributes to Carpaccio four more paintings and two more drawings. Two of the pictures, Sir William Farrer's *tondi* (Nos. 132 and 134), we have already seen to be by Montagna. Lord Battersea's "St. Bernardino" (No. 246) is not by Carpaccio. Mrs. Horner's "Allegorical Scene" (No. 68) is, as is proved by the general tone, the types, the hands, the draperies, and the landscape, a work by Michele da Verona, whose frequent good fortune it has been to attain Nirvana under the name of Carpaccio. Sir C. Robinson's drawing of a "Man with a Staff" (No. 323) is too feeble for Carpaccio, and the same holds true of Mr. G. Donaldson's "Figure of a Man" (No. 333).

XII.

Carpaccio was not, of course, the only follower Gentile Bellini had, but he is the only one of import-

---

[1] The identical figure recurs in a "Birth of the Virgin" at the Lochis Gallery in Bergamo, there ascribed to Carpaccio, by whom it was not painted, although designed.

ance represented in this exhibition, Bartolommeo
Veneto being not only an inferior artist, but of a later
generation, and subject to so many influences beside
Gentile's, that our best plan will be to treat him, not
at this point, but later. We shall therefore turn now
to Gentile's brother, GIOVANNI—*the* Bellini—whom
fate has dealt with more indulgently, the bulk of his
work having come down to us. Indeed, were we to
trust all existing catalogues, the number of his pictures
would be legion! In this exhibition alone, for example, some eighteen or nineteen works are attributed
to him. Of these, only three, as a matter of fact, are
by him—this proportion of about one to six being
the usual ratio of genuine Bellinis to merely attributed
pictures! Basaiti, as we have already seen, is responsible for three of these so-called Bellinis (Nos.
107, 167 and 169, all belonging to Mrs. Benson);
Rondinelli was the author of two others (Nos. 2 and
103); Catena of two more (Nos. 84 and 251); Rocco
Marconi, perhaps, of three (Nos. 19, 111 and 149);
while one, a "Madonna" (No. 26, lent by Lady
Lindsay), may be by Filippo Mazzola, whom we have
already encountered as the possible author of the
"Veronica" (No. 10). Another "Bellini," a Holy
Family (No. 81) is, as we have seen, by Speranza;
another still (No. 168) is a copy of the Castle Howard
"Circumcision"; and finally, the "Christoforo Moro,"
belonging to Lord Rosebery (No. 63), is a valueless
work, of no assignable character. Of the drawings
ascribed to Bellini, Sir C. Robinson's "Head of a
Young Man" (No. 347) seems to be the achievement
of some Venetian schoolboy, and Mr. G. Donaldson's
"Head of a Man" (No. 336) is not even Venetian,
being obviously by Leonardo's early assistant at
Milan, Ambrogio da Predis.

We must now examine all these pictures in connec-

tion with their real authors, and, first of all the three
genuine Bellinis. The earliest of these (No. 67) is
Dr. J. P. Richter's[1] half-length figure of the Virgin,
who bends slightly over, adoring the Child lying fast
asleep on a parapet before her. It is a quiet composition, severe, yet tender in feeling. The Madonna
is solidly constructed, the colouring is light and pleasant. The landscape recalls some of Bellini's very
earliest works, such as the " Transfiguration" and
the " Dead Christ" (with the forged monogram of
Dürer), both in the Correr Museum at Venice. The
contours throughout are timid, as might be expected
in a very early work such as this, and it is this earli-
ness that may account for the awkward drawing of
the Child, as it is hardly probable that a master would
leave such an important part of his work to a pupil,
when he himself had executed the rest. Next in date
to this " Madonna" stands (No. 119), Mr. Ludwig
Mond's pathetic picture of the " Dead Christ sup-
ported by two Angels," the noblest of all Bellini's
versions of this subject, with the exception, possibly,
of the kindred picture at Berlin (No. 28). The angels
are of almost the precise type of the Child in the
" Madonna with the Greek inscription" of the Brera
(No. 261), and the Greek inscription, as well as the
general technique of Mr. Mond's picture also recall
the Brera Madonna. They were probably painted
at about the same time, somewhere towards 1475.
The third and last genuine Bellini of this exhibition
must have been painted at least seven years later.
It is the impressive (although somewhat retouched)
" Madonna" (No. 79, signed IOANNES BELLINVS)
which recently passed from the Eastlake collection
into the hands of Mr. Ludwig Mond. Both the
Virgin and the Child recall the types Giovanni made

[1] Now belonging to Mr. Theo. M. Davis, of Newport, R. I.

use of before his " S. Giobbe and Frari " altar-pieces,
such, for instance, as we find in the " Madonna " in
the Venice Academy (No. 612), and the earlier of
the two Madonnas in the Morelli collection at Bergamo.

XIII.

While discussing the Basaitis signed with the name
of Bellini, I explained these signatures, it will be remembered, as being a sort of trade-mark of the Bellini factory.   The first assistant known to us who
seems to have been thus privileged to put the master's
name on his own pictures, was the Ravenese NICCOLO
RONDINELLI, of whose twenty-five works known to
me, a fair proportion bear the inscription IOANNES
BELLINVS.   A good instance is the " Madonna " lent
to this exhibition by Louisa, Lady Ashburton (No.
103), signed in the orthodox way, IOANNES BELLINVS P.
In this picture the draperies, which seem to be made
of paper, the colouring, the types, the big-bellied,
curly-haired child, all agree, detail for detail, with
Rondinelli's perfectly authenticated works at Rome,
Forlì, Ravenna and Milan.   An equally indisputable
Rondinelli is the pretty " Portrait of a Boy " (No. 2,
lent by Captain Holford), where the soft, humid look,
as well as the drawing and colour, betray unmistakably the style of Rondinelli.   That it could not be by
Bellini seems to have struck some connoisseur of the
distant past, for one of its former owners had the
marble ledge in front of this bust inscribed with the
indignant protest : " OPVS BELLINI IOANNIS VENETI NON
ALITER."
    Judging from most of his pictures signed Bellini,
Rondinelli must have been Giovanni's assistant be-

fure 1500. After that date he retired to Ravenna, and there became a sort of apostle of Venetian art *in partibus*, succeeding only in helping to deck out work of such dullards as Palmezzano and the Zaganellis, with some of the less desirable trappings imported from Venice. In his own pictures, painted at home, Rondinelli gives more than one sign of having come, during his stay in Venice, under the influence of Cima, and we have in one of the pictures here an example of this style. No. 143, a "Madonna and Child with SS. Catherine and Bartholomew," lent by Sir B. Samuelson, is actually attributed to Cima himself, although it is clearly a Rondinelli of a late period, with a style remotely suggesting Cima, although Bellinesque enough. Of Rondinelli's influence as a disseminator of Venetian art in the Romagna we have an interesting proof in Mrs. Benson's " Adoration of the Magi " (No. 74), signed BALDASAR FORLIVIENSI PINSIT—a picture which reveals its author, Baldassare da Forlì, as a tenth-rate painter, who churns together the mannerisms of Rondinelli and Palmezzano.

XIV.

FRANCESCO BISSOLO held much the same relation to Giovanni Bellini after 1500 that Rondinelli had held before, and it is a question which one of these two assistants was the feebler and more dependent. As for Bissolo, Messrs. Crowe and Cavalcaselle have aptly described his style as Sassoferrato-ish, and himself as the " Lo Spagna of Venice." They have not, however, so well understood his evolution. Noting the striking resemblance between his " Annunciation," now belonging to Mrs. Robert Benson,

PORTRAIT OF A YOUTH

and here exhibited (No. 35, signed FRANCISCVS BIS
SOLO), and certain pictures of Catena, they therefore
concluded that it was Bissolo's earliest work, starting, it seems, with the purely *à priori* assumption
that Bissolo was Catenesque before rather than after
he was Bellinesque. To this theory there is the insurmountable objection that Catena himself did not
acquire the manner which Bissolo is imitating in the
" Annunciation "—the manner which appears in the
way of painting the chamber, the landscape, and
the general scheme of colour—until his later years,
when Giovanni Bellini was already dead.[1] Incapable
of doing anything for himself, Bissolo always had to
lean on somebody, and Bellini being dead, on whom
could he lean so well as on the one painter who,
while not ignoring the new, yet remained faithful to
the old traditions, through which he himself was
never able to break—I mean on Vincenzo Catena ?
In his earlier, his purely Bellinesque manner, we see
Bissolo in a feeble but pleasantly coloured and otherwise inoffensive picture, a " Madonna with SS. Paul
and Catherine"(No. 155, lent by Mr. Ludwig Mond).
This work partakes of the precise character of the
picture by Bissolo still attributed to Bellini in the
Redentore at Venice, in type recalling, indeed, that
great master's San Zaccaria altar-piece of 1505, soon
after which it may have been painted.

---

[1] A further confirmation of this "Annunciation" being a late
picture rather than an early one, is the Italian, or half-Italian,
form of the signature the Latin form being *de rigueur* during
Giambellino's lifetime.

XV.

Suggestive of Bissolo in sentiment and colour, but of altogether superior character, are three pictures in this exhibition, all ascribed to Bellini, and all of them, if I mistake not, by the same hand. The " Virgin and Child " (No. 111, signed IOANNES BELLINVS), belonging to Sir Michael Shaw Stewart, is a charming panel of delicate sentiment, and refined, very blonde amber colouring. The same colouring and the same style of landscape reappear in one of the most delightful portraits of the Venetian school (No. 149, belonging to Mr. J. P. Carrington),—the bust of an alert, self-possessed, sympathetic, youngish man, with bushy brown hair, wearing a black cap and a black coat slashed with white—in conception not unworthy of Bellini himself, although widely different from him. In Lord Northbrook's " Madonna " (No. 19, signed IOANNES BELLINVS) with its exquisite landscape, we find the same delicacy of sentiment, and the same beautiful ambered lights. " A replica of the central group of a picture in the Redentore at Venice," says the catalogue. Quite so : the compositions are identical, but the execution is not. In this respect, as well as in the blondness of the hair, in the slight difference of axis to the eyes, and in the landscape, Lord Northbrook's " Madonna " stands much closer to a " Madonna," identical in composition, in the Strasburg Gallery (No. 221, photographed by Mathias Gerschel, Strasburg), signed ROCVS DE MARCHONIB.[1] It is to

---

[1] Another version of the same " Madonna," almost identical in every touch of the two figures may be seen at Breslau (No. 187). Reproduced in the illustrated catalogue of the Schlesisches Museum.

ROCCO MARCONI (?)

Dixon Photo.]   [Mr. J. P. Carrington.

PORTRAIT OF A MAN

this hitherto little known painter, ROCCO MARCONI, that I venture to ascribe the three pictures we have been discussing. Thus far he has passed as a mere imitator of Palma and Paris Bordone, and in his later years he doubtless deserved this bad reputation. In the Strasburg " Madonna," however, we see him starting from Bellini, but with a tendency of his own towards a very blond colouring—a tendency which we find amply developed in his masterpiece, the "Deposition from the Cross" of the Venice Academy (No. 166). Delicate and refined as is Mr. Carrington's portrait, the faces of the dead Christ and of the Virgin will bear comparison with it ; and as to its greater spirit, this would not be the first instance of a painter surpassing his usual self in portraiture (cf. Cordeliaghi and Girolamo Santacroce in their portraits in the Poldi-Pezzoli Museum at Milan). A further confirmation of my hypothesis may be found in still another work exhibited here. It is the full-length figure of the " Saviour," ascribed to Cima (No. 23, lent by Mr. Charles Butler). Although the figure certainly is copied from Cima's " Saviour " at Dresden, the execution and the landscape clearly betray Marconi's hand, as we know it in his pictures at Venice—not only the " Deposition " already mentioned, but the works in San Cassiano and San Giovanni e Paolo as well. Now careful scrutiny reveals more than one point of likeness between this " Saviour " and the three other pictures I have ventured to ascribe to Rocco Marconi. Nor are these the only pictures in London in which I recognize the same hand, presumably that of Rocco. Others are the pretty landscape, called a Giorgione, belonging to Lord Ashburnham (now on exhibition at the " Old Masters," in Burlington House, No. 115), containing in the foreground two men fencing and another piping; and, finally, the picture in the National Gallery, representing the "Death of St. Peter Martyr" (No. 1252), signed Ioannes Bellinus, and executed in his *atelier*.[1]

XVI.

Rocco Marconi was already a painter belonging to a period of transition, and subject to other strong influences besides Bellini's. The two or three other painters whose works we have to examine before arriving at Giorgione also have the transitionary character and proneness to eclecticism (within the limits of the school) which characterize Marconi. The oldest and most important of these artists is VINCENZO CATENA, a personality of considerable weight in Venetian art, to whom scant justice has hitherto been awarded, most of his finest pictures still passing as Bellini's or Giorgione's. Unfortunately this is not the place for a reconstruction of his artistic personality, and, tempting as the subject is, I must content myself with a brief analysis of his eight pictures in the New Gallery, four of which, only, bear his name. The earliest of his works here is a large panel of ivory tone and ivory-like hardness, representing the Madonna with her hand on a Donor, recommended by St. John, while the Child glances at another Donor, overtowered by a female saint (No. 46, lent by Miss Hertz, signed VICENZIVS

---

[1] I let this paragraph on Marconi stand because what I say therein may be true, but I would have it taken as a suggestion, and with caution. Marconi's artistic personality remains incomplete and vague, and certainly has been confused with Beccaruzzi's.

CHAENA P.). The Madonna, in type, dress, and action, is the one which seems to have been in peculiar favour at the beginning of the sixteenth century, for she is found in Lotto, Basaiti, Marco Veneto, and in Catena more than once.[1] The St. John is surprisingly crude, a caricature of Cima's Baptist, as he appears in the " Madonna with SS. Paul and John," in the Venice Academy (No. 603), or in his Conegliano and Parma altar-pieces. The female saint is, however, almost agreeable, and in type she recalls Cima, as in the altar-pieces just mentioned (photographed by D. Anderson, Rome), and in his Munich " Madonna with St. Jerome and the Magdalen" (No. 1033). The Child, again, is like a caricature of Cima, particularly of such a Child as the one in the Berlin " Madonna and Donor" (No. 7). The ivory tone and ivory-like hardness also have a relation to Cima's technique, and in the landscape there is much to suggest Cima (witness the Berlin picture just mentioned), and Basaiti. In the portraits of the Donors, however, there is something of Gentile Bellini. Catena, then, as he reveals himself in this early work, is a feeble artist closely allied to Cima and less closely to another of Alvise Vivarini's pupils, to Basaiti, and at the same time somewhat influenced by Gentile.

The Liverpool picture here exhibited (No. 98, signed VINCENCIVS CHATENA F.), a " Madonna with SS. Nicholas of Bari, Francis, a female Saint, and a Donor," shows Catena in scarcely a better light. He appears (in the Francis especially) even more closely affiliated with the school of Alvise Vivarini, and he is here even cruder and harder and less interesting. Both these pictures belong to an early

[1] At Naples, Stuttgart, Berlin, Bergamo, and in the former Pourtalis collection respectively.

group, of which two other examples are in the Buda-
Pesth Gallery, and one in the Raczinski Collection
at Berlin.   Considerable advance is indicated in the
" Madonna with the Magdalen and St. Catherine"
(No. 123, lent by the Corporation of Glasgow, and
labelled " School of Giovanni Bellini "),[1] in both
expression and colour, if not in draughtsmanship.
The Child has the firmly-shut mouth so characteristic of Catena.   Here, for the first time, we
encounter the emerald green and the soft pinks that
make up so much of Catena's charm.   In such a
work as this he is already not far away from the
" Madonna with Saints " (No. 19) of Berlin, and on
the high road to such a masterpiece as the "Warrior
adoring the Infant Christ " of the National Gallery
(No. 234, called " School of Giovanni Bellini ").[2]

To about this period of Catena's career belongs a
ruined altar-piece, a " Madonna with two Saints and
a Donor," in the collection of Lord Ashburnham
(now exhibited at the " Old Masters" in Burlington
House, No. 116), whose authorship becomes clear
the moment we compare it with Catena's signed
altar-piece in the Ducal Palace at Venice.   It is
true that Lord Ashburnham's picture is inscribed
IOANNES BELLINVS, MCCCCCV., but this proves, if anything, no more than that in 1505 Catena, like Basaiti,
was also turning out pictures for Bellini's factory.   It
is to about this date—somewhat later rather than
earlier—that I would ascribe the famous Castle
Howard " Circumcision " (No. 84),[3] which still
enjoys the reputation of being Bellini's splendid
original of a large flock of copies scattered over the

---

[1] In the second edition of the authorized catalogue correctly
ascribed to Catena.
[2] Now at last ascribed to Catena.
[3] Now at the National Gallery.

length and breadth of Europe. True, this picture
is also signed IOANNES BELLINVS; but the types are
not Bellini's, and are in fact, strictly speaking, not
even Bellinesque. Where among Bellini's unquestionable works shall we find such a heavy-featured
Madonna, or one wearing a kerchief such as she
wears here? Where such a Child? I venture to
say nowhere. On the other hand, the forms—hands,
ears, and folds of drapery in particular—are clearly
Catena's. His also are the types, the Child being
remarkably like the one in his signed picture at
Buda-Pesth. As to the technique, so far as its very
bad condition permits any judgment, it certainly is
much more like that of Catena's authentic works than
of Bellini's, and the colouring, with its vivid pinks
and greens, will be sought for in vain in Bellini,
while it is highly characteristic of Catena. It seems
therefore safe to assert that in this "Circumcision"
we have a work by Catena and no other, and a
work, moreover, of transition from pictures such as
those we have already examined to works such as
we shall take up presently. That Bellini may have
painted this subject is possible, nay, highly probable, and it is likely that the Castle Howard "Circumcision" is a free version of some such original;
but the point to be remembered is that this is not
Bellini's original, but at the most a version by Catena.
Nor is this the only version of the same composition
from Catena's own hand. Another, also provided
with Bellini's signature, and dated 1511, was in the
Goldschmidt collection at Paris. Moreover, the
best copies of this subject, such as the one in the
Doria Palace at Rome, and the one exhibited here
under Bellini's name (No. 168, lent by Mr. John
Stogdon), are pretty exact copies of the Castle
Howard version, which would rather point to the

conclusion that this is the only original that ever existed, and that Catena himself, therefore, actually invented the composition.

In the four remaining pictures by Catena here exhibited, we see him in his last phase—a phase in which he reveals himself as an artist of extraordinary suppleness of mind, never too old to learn, nor, what is more wonderful, too old to feel afresh, to appreciate new ideals and new sentiments. He is Giorgionesque in his last phases, not slavishly, but tactfully, adopting as much of Giorgione as he really can make his own, and never merely copying him. It is not in his types—always the easiest thing for a copyist to lay hold of—but in the more subtle qualities of a heightened sense of beauty, a greater refinement of line, enchantment of colour, and magic of feeling that he gives evidence of contact with Giorgione. Of the four pictures here belonging to Catena's Giorgionesque phase, one only is attributed to him, Mr. J. P. Heseltine's "Holy Family" (No. 161). In this work the types, the draperies, the colours, and the painting of the foliage are all startlingly like the "Warrior adoring the Infant Christ," a picture which, despite the phenomenal agreement of Morelli with Crowe and Cavalcaselle as to its being a Catena, is nevertheless refused that attribution by the authorities of the National Gallery.[1] Delightful as is Mr. Heseltine's "Holy Family," it is even surpassed by Lord Brownlow's "Nativity" (No. 251, ascribed to Giovanni Bellini). Few pictures of the Venetian school have a more idyllic charm and loveliness; few are executed with greater daintiness. All the woodwork is as delicately painted as in Catena's "St. Jerome" in the National Gallery (No. 234). The effects of light are even more poetical than in Mr. Heseltine's picture.

[1] Now accepted.

CATENA

[*Earl Brownlow.*

THE NATIVITY

The kneeling shepherd is a Venetian gentleman of almost Lottesque refinement. There can be no doubt whatever that this "Nativity" is by Catena. The Virgin, whose drapery, by the way, is most characteristic of the master, is of the type of the St. Christina in Catena's altar-piece in Santa Maria Mater Domini, at Venice ; the Child so fast asleep is absolutely identical with the one in the undisputed "Madonna and Saints" at Berlin ; the painting of the foliage is precisely the same as in the National Gallery "Adoring Warrior," or as in Mr. Heseltine's picture, and the same boy who is seen approaching in Lord Brownlow's "Nativity" appears also in the middle distance of Mr. Heseltine's "Holy Family."

Even more Giorgionesque in outward characteristics, as, for instance, in the drapery and colouring, although by no means so close to Giorgione in quality of magic, is Mrs. Benson's small "Holy Family" (No. 148, attributed to Giorgione). The type of the Virgin is thoroughly Catenesque, and although the large sweep of the draperies recalls Giorgione, it is identical in flow with the draperies of the kneeling shepherd and of St. Joseph in Lord Brownlow's picture, while the smaller folds of the Virgin's skirt are such as may be found almost everywhere in Catena. In the Brownlow "Nativity" Catena goes as far as he can in the natural, unforced assimilation of the Giorgionesque. In Mrs. Benson's "Holy Family" he is already a trifle on the downward path, and he appears in a still later, and almost degenerate phase in such a picture as the "Christ at Emmaus" in the Bergamo Gallery (Carrara, No. 11, photographed by R. Lotze, Verona), where the old and the new seem no longer to assimilate but to remain more or less apart and episodic. In the New Gallery we see Catena in this phase in Mr. Charles Butler's "Christ

and the Woman of Samaria" (No. 154, attributed to
Altobello Melone), a picture which in colour and in
form of hand and ear is characteristic of Catena's late
works.   In types and draperies it is identical with
the "Christ at Emmaus," but of an even more unequal quality, awkward enough to suggest Cariani.
This suggestion is enforced by a certain touch of
Palma in the figures, with whom Catena may well
have come in contact.

XVII.

Catena was already a combiner. More of the charm
which lies in his fine last works is due to his almost
unconscious combination of the styles of Alvise, the
Bellini, and Carpaccio, than one might think. In him
nature may have been trying her hand at a Giorgione,
but he was born perhaps a decade too early for success.
All that he failed to accomplish was left to be triumph-
antly carried out by Giorgione, who succeeded in
combining into an harmonious whole almost all of
what was best in the various schools of Venice, all
of Alvise, all of the Bellini, and all of Carpaccio that
could keep house together. Nor could this combination have been at all conscious, for we find it already
in his very earliest existing works, the "Judgment of
Solomon" and the "Trial of Moses."

Before turning, however, to the consideration of
the pictures in the New Gallery attributed to this most
fascinating of Venetian artists, we must mention the
works of two painters, both of whom were of that type
of people, common at all times and in every walk of
life—even in art criticism—who are a good generation
behind the most advanced people of their day.   In
future ages the opinions, practices and performances

Houlyer Photo.]   [Mrs. R. H. Benson.

MADONNA AND CHILD AND TWO ANGELS

of these *rétardataires* are almost always utterly forgotten, because our interest in the past is an interest in the forward and not in the backward activity of a period. Among these *rétardataires* there are various kinds : some are so because of unalloyed stupidity ; others because of vested interests ; and others still because of the picturesqueness of their own temperaments. We find a *rétardataire* of the first class in FRANCESCO SANTACROCE, and of the last, in BARTOLOMMEO VENETO, both of whom, younger than Giorgione, remained pre-Giorgionesque for thirty or forty years after his death.

By Francesco Santacroce, whose earliest known work is the Bergamo "Annunciation," dated 1504 (Carrara, No. 70), there are in the New Gallery two pictures. Mr. Charles Butler's "Virgin, Child, and Donor" (No. 12, attributed to Previtali[1]) has the types and colouring of Francesco Santacroce of about 1512. Mrs. Benson lends a "Marriage of St. Catherine" (No. 16), which is ascribed to Catena—were it really by Catena then there would be ample justification for ascribing the little "Holy Family" to Giorgione !— but which is by Francesco Santacroce in his maturest phase, as the landscape, the eyes of the St. Catherine, the golden amber tone, and the modelling throughout clearly prove.

The always picturesque Bartolommeo Veneto, who in his earliest known work, the Bergamo "Madonna" of 1505 (Lochis, No. 127), shows considerable affinity with the Bergamask painters, is represented here by more than one work. The earliest is a picture showing even closer affinities with the Bergamasks,

---

[1] There is one picture by Previtali in this exhibition, the "Portrait Group" (No. 293, lent by Mr. Archibald Stirling of Keir). Lord Northbrook's "Madonna and Saints" (No. 60) is by Girolamo Santacroce.

although painted some five or eight years later, the "Madonna with two Angels" (No. 11, lent by Mrs. Benson), and attributed to its real author. The face of the Madonna in this picture seems to be already that of the Jewess of German type, whom we find in Bartolommeo's signed picture in the Melzi collection at Milan—a woman represented in the act of breaking a ring with a hammer—some wedded Jessica with whom Bartolommeo may have played the part of Lorenzo. Very close to that picture stands another version of the same model, this time represented as "St. Catherine" (No. 8, lent by the Corporation of Glasgow). Her hair is less like twisted wire than in the Melzi portrait, but, on the other hand, she serves as a connecting link between the latter and the Frankfort "Courtesan" (No. 13), who, like the "St. Catherine," has her head engarlanded—and completes the demonstration, complete though it had been, that the Frankfort picture is by Bartolommeo. Even MM. Thode and Müntz would be won from their fond belief that the Frankfort "Courtesan" is by Dürer, if they compared it with the photographs of these other unquestionable works. Still by Bartolommeo, although attributed to Sebastiano del Piombo, is the fine portrait of a "Venetian Noble" wearing a large velvet hat (No. 61, lent by M. Somzée). Here we have the painter in a later and much higher phase, in his grey manner, exactly as we see him in the Dresden "Salome" (No. 292), and in the portrait attributed to Beltraffio in the Ambrosiana at Milan.[1]

Coming at last to the centre point of Venetian art, to the shadowy, fluctuating, half-mythical figure of GIORGIONE, concerning whom there seems to be so

---

[1] The abuse of new names appears in the utterly unwarranted attribution to Bartolommeo of a portrait belonging to Mr. George Salting (No. 30).

MUSICIANS

little certainty that it may well be said : Every critic
has his own private Giorgione—coming, at last, to
him, we find that the catalogue, with becoming im-
modesty, ascribes to him no less than eighteen distinct
items. Well, their private Giorgione is, I hasten to
say, not mine. Mine makes up in quality what he
loses in quantity. But let us now examine these
eighteen hypothetical Giorgiones.

Two of them we have met with already, Mrs.
Benson's Catena (No. 148), and Mr. Butler's Buonconsiglio (No. 275). Lord Malmesbury's " Judgment
of Paris " (No. 29) is a wretched copy after a picture
attributed to Giorgione, but probably by Polidoro
Lanzani, in the Palazzo Albuzio at Venice (photographed by Brusa, Venice).[1] Sir Edward Burne-
Jones' " Europa " (No. 94) is the merest wreck, and
could never, at the best, have been more than a daub
by Andrea Schiavone. Louisa, Lady Ashburton's
" Landscape with Figures " (No. 147) is of more than
doubtful antiquity. The " Musicians " (No. 99), lent
by the Corporation of Glasgow, has but slight connection with Giorgione, although it is a pleasant picture of considerable merit. As to its authorship I
have no clue whatever.[2] Sir William Farrer's " Three
Ages " (No. 82) is obviously a copy, probably by
Polidoro Lanzani, after Titian's original in Bridge-
water House.[3]

Perhaps of all the " Giorgiones " here, the one that
is best placed and that attracts the most attention is

[1] This, in turn, is only a copy of some now lost original by
Giorgione, or, more probably, Titian. Other copies exist at Dresden and Christiania.

[2] It is by Romanino in his golden phase.

[3] Other pictures here, by this brilliant follower of Titian and
Bonifazio, are four works ascribed to Titian, and one unattributed.
The " Titians " are Sir William Farrer's " Holy Family with two
Donors " (No. 179) ; the Glasgow " Holy Family and St. Dorothy

Louisa, Lady Ashburton's "Portrait of a Lady Professor of Bologna" (No. 91). To begin with, this portrait is neither of a lady, nor of a Professor, nor of Bologna. It represents a smooth shaven, sentimental young man, dressed in the costume of the time, with bushy, curly dark hair. His left hand rests on a skull before him. The tone of this picture is between ivory and amber—a tone with which we are familiar in the works of the hitherto but little known, although prolific painter, great colourist and poor artist, Bernardino Licinio. Characteristic of him is also the cranium of this young man, the pose of the head, and the extreme awkwardness in the drawing of the mouth. As to the hand, never was one hand more like another hand than the one here is to that of St. Elizabeth in the Borghese "Santa Conversazione" (No. 171, photographed by Anderson, Rome, No. 4240). The dark blue velvet of his dress is identical not only in colour but in folds with the sleeve of St. Catherine in the same picture. That Licinio and no other was the author of this portrait is, in fact, proved more and more by every comparison with his other works that may be made. And this, by the way, is not his only picture in the New Gallery, although his name does not appear anywhere in the catalogue. In Captain Holford's "Adoration of the Shepherds" (No. 224, ascribed to Bonafazio), we have Licinio in his Bonifaziesque phase, and dazzling as a colourist—a phase known to us by a series of pictures of which Duke Scotti's at Milan are good examples. In nearly the

(No. 133); Captain Holford's "Holy Family" (No. 158), a replica of a Polidoro in the Louvre (No. 1580, there ascribed also to Titian); and Lord Battersea's "Madonna with the Infant John (No. 227). Polidoro's masterpiece—a pleasant fusion of much that is charming—but charming only—in Titian and Bonifazio, is the unascribed "Madonna with St. Catherine and the Archangel Michael" (No. 225), belonging to Mrs. R. H. Benson.

LICINIO

A LADY PROFESSOR OF THE UNIVERSITY OF BOLOGNA

same phase we see him in a " Portrait of a Man " also belonging to Captain Holford (No. 194, ascribed to Palma Vecchio) ; and we have him again, this time in his Pordenonesque manner, in a wretched " Portrait of a Senator," ascribed to Sebastiano del Piombo (No. 191, also belonging to Captain Holford).

Much closer to Giorgione than this " Lady Professor" stands Lord Lansdowne's " Concert" (No. 110), although it is far enough away, as far away, in fact, as Cariani is from Giorgione. The picture is thus described in the catalogue : " A young man with a viola across his lap, is seated under a tree ; opposite to him are two young women, one holding an open book ; all are seated on the banks of a stream ; on the other side of the stream, which occupies the middle distance, are houses with a hilly landscape." It is impossible to read even this bare description without visualizing something very romantic, if one has any acquaintance with the Giorgionesque way of treating such a subject. We feel here, although to a less degree, the high idyllic charm of that most wonderful of all painted idylls, Giorgione's " Fête Champêtre " of the Louvre. Looking closer, however, we find that the colour scheme is by no means Giorgionesque, but Palmesque, the bright yellows and the greens being essentially Bergamask. But Palma himself is excluded from the authorship of this picture, not only because he never catches so much of Giorgione's spirit, but because he never draws so badly, or uses so thin a vehicle. In all these points this "Concert" is thoroughly characteristic of Cariani's manner at a time when he appears to have been absorbed in studying Giorgione, while changing over from the style of Lotto and his slow and thin medium to that of Palma and his fluid, thick medium. As to the spirit of the picture, we have Cariani in precisely

this phase in a canvas at Bergamo, " A woman playing and a Shepherd asleep" (Lochis, No. 146).
Even the forms and folds are thoroughly characteristic of Cariani, and peculiar to him are the short
noses and the way the faces are modelled, especially
the youth's face, whose modelling is identical with
that in the Vienna " Bravo " (No. 240), the Borghese
" Madonna" (No. 164), and the Louvre " Santa
Conversazione " (No. 1135) still attributed to Giorgione, although obviously by Cariani.[1]

Of the remaining works attributed to Giorgione,
only one is a painting, the rest being drawings. But
that one is, in my opinion, by Giorgione himself. It
is the "Head of a Shepherd" (No. 112) from the
Hampton Court Gallery. A recent writer on the
pictures of this collection has spoken of it in words
that I cannot do better than quote :—" The face is so

---

[1] Besides the three paintings attributed to Cariani in the catalogue—Mr. Salting's admirable replica of the " Portrait of a
Noble " (No. 144), (the version in the Casa Suardi at Bergamo is
even better), Captain Holford's crude "Portrait of a Man " (No.
27), and Mrs. Benson's " Portrait of a Man " (No. 230)—beside
these there are on exhibition another picture entirely by Cariani,
and three more which he executed in great part, although they
were begun by Palma. The work entirely by Cariani is Mrs. Benson's " Holy Family and Donor " (No. 9, ascribed to Romanino).
Here the Madonna is of the type in the Louvre so-called " Giorgione "; and the Donor is strikingly like the portrait that used to
be in the Leyland collection (under the name of Giorgione), which
now belongs to M. Aynard, of Paris. The landscape—a view of
Bergamo, seen from Ponteranica—the loose index finger of the
Madonna, the high light on St. Joseph's forehead, and the hot
colouring, are all characteristic of Cariani. Three " Sante Con-
versazioni " (No. 92, lent by Mr. Wickham Flower ; No. 128, lent
by the Glasgow Corporation ; and No. 221, lent by Mrs. Benson)
—all attributed to Palma—were, it is true, laid in by that master,
but left (probably at his death) in various stages of incompleteness,
and finished by Cariani. The share of each painter in these works
is perfectly distinguishable.

[*Marquess of Lansdowne.*

THE CONCERT

SHEPHERD AND LADY

CARIANI

HOLY FAMILY AND DONORS

[*Mrs. R. H. Benson.*

radiantly beautiful that even retouching and blackening have not been able to hide the fine oval, the exquisite proportions, the warm eyes, the sweet mouth, the soft waving hair, and the easy poise of the head."[1] This is not too enthusiastic a description of the supreme beauty and poetic charm of this wonderful head. I can scarcely hope that many of those who see it in the wretched place given to it in the New Gallery will feel so ecstatic about it as I do; but then they have not had my good fortune of studying it under the full light of the sun.

This picture, whose first discoverer was Morelli, is no longer accepted as a Giorgione by the Morellians. If their master, they say, had seen it in a good light, he never would have taken it for a Giorgione. It is easy to say such a thing now that Morelli is dead; but its being disputed compels me to defend it. Let us in the first place turn to a morphological comparison of this head with those few pictures by Giorgione that are least called in question.

Perhaps the most striking resemblance of all is that of this head to the head of the " Sleeping Venus " at Dresden, the same broad face, broad brow, the same modelling of the lids, the same shape of nose and mouth. With the " Knight of Malta " in the Uffizi it has in common the broad brow, and the precise way of opening the eyes, and of modelling the lids; with the Loschi "Christ bearing the Cross (at Vicenza),[2] it has in common the eyelids, the mouth, and the folds of the drapery; with the Castelfranco and Madrid " Madonnas" it has in common the mouth; with the Berlin portrait there is also a great likeness in the folds (cf. particularly the R. sleeve), and in the

---

[1] Mary Logan. "Guide to the Italian Pictures at Hampton Court." The Kyrle Society, 1894 (Price 2d.), p. 13.

[2] Now Mrs. Gardner's, Boston, U.S.A.

mouth ; and, finally, the Hampton Court "Shepherd" shares with all of Giorgione's universally
accepted works, the dome-shaped cranium.

What, then, is the fatal flaw in this picture ? Alas !
it is the hand holding the flute, which, as it happens,
is not at all unlike Giorgione's hand—*he*, by the way,
has a number of characteristic hands—but which is,
unfortunately, in the opinion of some critics, more
like Palma's hand, and, in the opinion of others, more
like Pordenone's. Therefore, despite the diametrical
opposition in every other morphological detail, and,
above all, in spirit, between this head and any and
every authenticated work by either Palma or Pordenone, the fatal hand condemns it to be a work of
one or the other of these inferior painters. This,
truly, is being more Morellian by very much than
Morelli himself !

But let us inquire a little more closely into this
question of the hand. In so far as Giorgione has
at all a stereotyped hand, what is its most peculiar
characteristic ? It is the tendency to give great
prominence and looseness to the forefinger, as we
see in the " Knight of Malta," and, to an exaggerated
degree in the Pallas of the " Evander and Aeneas "
(alias the " Three Magi ") of Vienna. Now, what
is the greatest peculiarity in the hand of the " Shepherd " ? Precisely this looseness and prominence
of the forefinger. In so far as the hand is unsatis-
factory in other respects, I think it is due to the
condition of the picture. There is, at all events,
nothing surprising in the fact that people who exploited Giorgione so much as did Palma and Pordenone, should have adopted some obvious manner-
ism—always the easiest thing to imitate—of the
supreme master.

But if we really must make the hand the palladium

GIORGIONE

THE SHEPHERD BOY

of identity, what shall we say of the now commonly
accepted "Portrait of a Young Man" at Buda-
Pesth ?   That masterpiece has a hand quite unlike
any other in Giorgione, but very close to Cariani's
most characteristic hand, and closer still to the hands
in such a Pordenone as the altar-piece in the Cathedral of Cremona.   Were one to go by the hand, the
Buda-Pesth portrait would certainly be a Pordenone,
particularly as in no other accepted work do we find
Giorgione so grey in tone and so self-consciously
melancholic as in this portrait, while this spirit is
close to Pordenone, and this grey tone is singularly
like the Cremona altar-piece.   Nevertheless, I cannot
let myself be run away with by these outer resemblances, nor even the resemblances of spirit, because
I know Pordenone, and I know that great though
he was, he was utterly inadequate to such an achievement as the Buda-Pesth portrait.   Its likenesses to
Pordenone I account for in this way. Of the various
sides of a supreme master, each follower finds one
that appeals more strongly than any other to his
own temperament.   Pordenone, inclined to be
haughty and over self-esteeming, found himself
set in vibration by the Buda-Pesth "Young Man,"
and naturally said to himself, "*This* is what I want
to say about things, and this is therefore the way to
say it."   And thereupon he began to exploit that
one segment of Giorgione's art.

Now that I have done what I could to prove by
internal evidence of a morphological nature that the
" Shepherd with a Pipe " is by Giorgione ; now that
I have explained how it may happen that the hand
should remind some people of Palma and some of
Pordenone, let us see what outside evidence there
may be for the authenticity of this picture.

That subjects akin to this were treated by Giorgione, we know well from the Anonimo, who saw in the Palace of Zuane Ram "the head of a boy who holds in his hand an arrow," and "the head of a shepherd who holds in his hand a flute."[1]   But we have something even more precise.   The self-same head that occurs in the Hampton Court "Shepherd" is found in a picture in the Imperial Gallery at Vienna (No. 213), which represents "the young David whose luxuriant hair falls down on both sides of his face.   He wears a breastplate "—the catalogue continues—"and holds the sword of Goliath in his R. hand, while with his L. he places the giant's head on the parapet behind which he is standing."[2]   Now this picture is obviously a copy (let anyone who is tempted to think the Hampton Court "Shepherd" only a copy, compare it, by the way, with the Vienna picture !), but it is an old copy, for we find it mentioned in the collection of the Archduke Leopold William at Brussels.   Yet, copy though it be, it is of interest to us, for if we have the imagination to supply this copy with a quality of execution adequate to the quality of conception, we arrive at nothing less than a masterpiece by Giorgione himself.   And here Vasari comes to our aid.   Among the pictures he saw in the house of the Patriarch of Aquileia, he mentions as being by Giorgione "a David with a shock of hair, such as used to be worn in those days, down to the shoulders, lively and coloured, so as to seem flesh and blood.   He has an arm and the breast covered with armour, and holds the head of Goliath."[3]   Allowing for the difference in exactness between the casual Vasari and the scrupulous accuracy of the modern cataloguer,

[1] Anonimo, ed. Frizzoni, p. 208.
[2] E. v. Engerth, Vol. i., p. 171.
[3] Vasari, ed. Sansoni, iv., p. 93.

Vasari's and Von Engerth's descriptions certainly apply to the same picture.. The Vienna "David" is, therefore, indubitably a copy after a Giorgione. Now, as the head in the Vienna picture is identical with that of the Hampton Court "Shepherd," it follows that the latter is also an original, or a copy after an original by Giorgione. As to which of the two it may be, that is no longer a matter of quantitative reasoning, and argument concerning it is, therefore, useless. All that can be done is to beg the competent in this matter, as I have already done, to compare the one with the other, and to note the gulf between the quality of the "David" and that of the "Shepherd," giving them only this further hint, that Giorgione, while always supreme in his conceptions, did not live long enough to acquire a perfection of draughtsmanship and chiaroscuro equally supreme, and that, consequently, there is not a single universally-accepted work of his which is absolutely free from the reproaches of the academic pedant.

In my eagerness to vindicate for Giorgione this wonderful head, I forgot to speak of a portrait bust attributed to this master, of exquisite quality, but deplorably bad preservation, which belongs to Mr. A. H. Savage Landor (No. 15). It may have been a work by the young Titian, or else only a copy after such a work, the copy by Polidoro Lanzani.

Of the seven drawings ascribed to Giorgione only one is really by him, the early sketch for the martyrdom of a saint, from the Chatsworth collection (No. 319), reproduced in Morelli.[1] Of the remainder,

---

[1] "Italian Masters : Munich and Dresden Galleries." English Translation, p. 225.

(N.B.—The drawings from Chatsworth, No. 838-883, are not referred to in this essay, having been added to the exhibition at a date subsequent to the writer's visit to England.)

Nos. 312, 334, 342, and 348 are nothing in particular; the red chalk sketch for a " Death of Peter Martyr " (No. 320, also from Chatsworth) is Pordenonesque; and a " Saint Preaching " (No. 321, from the same collection) is of the school of Gentile Bellini, possibly by his follower, Benedetto Diana.

We have now ended our survey of the pre-Titianesque works exhibited in the New Gallery. A detailed examination of the sixteenth century Venetians would reveal an even greater number of questionable attributions, and would entail the resuscitation of many wholly or half-forgotten painters— the real authors of a large proportion of the pictures here which pass under the ringing names of Titian, Bonifazio, Palma, Paris Bordone, and Paolo Veronese. Such a study would require not a pamphlet but a book, and as it would chiefly concern artists whose names thus far have been but seldom heard, it could not hope to have the least interest for any but specialists.

Index

INDEX

Alamanno, Pietro, 103.
  London, Sir William Farrer,
    103.
Amico di Sandro, 46-69.
  Altenburg, 62.
  Bergamo, 61.
  Berlin, 59.
  Buda Pesth, 57, 58.
  Chantilly, Musée Condé, 55,
    56.
  Florence, Corsini Gallery, 47.
  Cenacolo di Foligno, 59.
  Pitti, 52, 62.
  Torrigiani Collection (form-
    er), 55.
  Uffizi, 48.
  Horsmonden, Mrs. Austen, 48.
  London, Mr. Robert Benson,
    57.
  National Gallery, 54, 57, 58.
  South Kensington Museum
    (formerly Ionides), 60.
  Meiningen, 57.
  Milan, Prince Trivulzio, 63.
  New Battle, Lord Lothian, 51.
  Paris, The Louvre, 49, 52, 63.
  Philadelphia, U.S.A., Mr.
    Johnson, 64.
  Rome, Count Gregori Stro-
    ganoff, 59.
  St. Petersburg, Leuchtenberg
    Collection, 63.
  Turin, 48, 49.
  Vienna, Prince Lichtenstein,
    55, 56, 63.

Andrea del Sarto, 40, 49.
Angelico, Fra, 4.
Antonello da Messina, 105, 106,
  107, 108.
  Venice, 107.

Baldassare da Forli, 124.
  Mrs. Robert Benson, 124.
Basaiti, 110-113.
  Alnwick, 114.
  Liverpool (110).
  London, National Gallery,
    111.
  Mrs. R. Benson, 110, 111,
    113.
  Mr. G. Salting, 110.
  Padua, 112.
Bassano, Francesco the Elder,
  116.
  The Duke of Norfolk, 116.
Beccaruzzi, 83, 128.
  London, Captain Holford,
    91.
  Lord Powerscourt, 91.
Bellini, Gentile, 112, 118, 119.
  London, Mr. Ludwig Mond,
    119.
  Oxford, University Galleries
    (118).
Bellini, Giovanni, 18, 121-123,
  131.
  Alnwick, 114.
  Bergamo, 123.
  London, Mr. L. Mond, 122.
  Dr. J. P. Richter 122.

Bellini, Giovanni, *continued*.
  Milan, Brera, 122.
  Newport, U.S.A., Mr. Theo.
    M. Davis, 122.
  Venice, Academy, 123.
    Museo Correr, 122.
Bellini, Jacopo, 93, 94, 95.
  Lovere, 119.
Bianchi, 28, 29, 30.
  Paris, 29.
Bissolo, 124, 125.
  London, Mrs. R. Benson,
    124.
    Mr. L. Mond, 125.
  Venice, Redentore, 125.
Bonsignori.
  London, Dr. J. P. Richter,
    96.
  Milan, Poldi Pezzoli, 112.
Botticelli, 9, 40, 46, 65.
  Berlin, 10, 16, 46.
  Florence, Uffizi, 46, 47.
  London, National Gallery, 52.
  Rome, Prince Chigi, 46, 47,
    48.
Botticini.
  Florence, Academy, 50.
Brunelleschi, 4, 7.
Brusasorci, Domenico.
  London, Lord Battersea, 9?.
Buonconsiglio (Mareschalco),
    116-118.
  Bergamo, 117.
  London, Mr. Charles Butler,
    118.
    Captain Holford, 118.
    Mr. T. Humphrey Ward,
      117.
  Rovigo, 117.
  Vicenza, S. Rocco, 117.
    Pinacoteca, 117.

Caprioli.
  Paris, Mme. C. de Rosen-
    berg, 91.

Caracci, 20, 21.
Cariani, 78, 79, 139, 140.
  Bergamo, 78, 140.
  Glasgow, 140.
  London, Mrs. R. Benson,
    140.
    Mr. Wickham Flower, 140.
    Lord Lansdowne, 139.
  Lyons, M. Aynard (formerly),
    139.
  Paris, the Louvre, 140.
  Vienna, 140.
Caroto.
  London, Mr. L. Mond, 113.
Carpaccio, 32, 119, 120.
  London, Mrs. R. Benson,
    120.
    Sir Charles Robinson, 120.
Castagno, 4, 8.
Catena.
  Ashridge, Lord Brownlow,
    132.
  Bergamo, 133.
  Berlin, 130, 133.
  Castle Howard, 130.
  Glasgow, 130.
  Liverpool, 129.
  London, Lord Ashburnham,
    130.
    Mrs. R. Benson, 133.
    Mr. Charles Butler, 134.
    Miss Hertz, 128.
    Mr. J. P. Heseltine, 132.
    National Gallery, 130, 131,
      132.
  Paris, Goldschmidt Collection
    (dispersed), 131.
  Rome, Doria Palace (131).
  Venice, Sta. Maria Mater
    Domini, 133.
Cima da Conegliano, 108-110,
    129.
  Ashridge, Lord Brownlow,
    108, 109.
  Dresden, 109.

Cima da Conegliano, *continued*.
London, Mr. L. Mond, 108,
109.
National Gallery, 108.
Richmond, Sir F. Cook (108).
Windsor, 110.
Cimabue, 4, 5, 6.
Cordeliaghi.
Milan, Poldi Pazzoli, 127.
Correggio, 20-45.
Berlin, 38, 43.
Dresden, 20-38, 42.
Florence, Uffizi, 31, 35, 42.
Hampton Court, 31.
London, Mr. R. Benson,
34.
Milan, Brera, 35.
Signor Crespi, 31, 34.
Signor Frizzoni, 31.
Municipal Museum, 31.
Munich, 35.
Naples, 42.
Paris, 29, 38, 45.
Parma, 42, 43, 44.
Pavia, 31.
Rome, Borghese, 38, 42.
Vienna, 38, 43.
Costa, 27, 28, 30, 33, 35, 40.
Credi, 110.
Crivelli, Carlo, 101-103.
Boston, U.S.A., Mrs. J. L.
Gardner, 102.
London.
Louisa, Lady Ashburton,
103.
Mrs. R. Benson, 102.
Mr. R. Crawshay, 103.
Lord Northbrook, 102, 103.
Maccrata, 102.
Massa Fermana, 102.
Richmond, Sir F. Cook,
102.
Crivelli, Vittorio.
London, Mr. S. Milner Gib-
son Cullum, 103.

Desiderio da Settignano, 4.
Diana, Benedetto.
Chatsworth, 146.
Domenichino, 21.
Donatello, 4, 8, 95.
Dosso Dossi, 30, 31, 32, 33, 34,
40, 41.
Dresden, 31, 33.
Rome, Borghese, 32, 35.
Duccio, 15.

Fabriano, Gentile da, 93.
Fasolo, G.
Brussels, M. Léon Somzée,
92.
Filippino Lippi, 65-67, 69.
Florence, Carmine, 66.
Corsini Gallery, 66.
Naples, 66.
Fra Filippo Lippi, 4, 95.
Florence, Uffizi, 46.
London, National Gallery, 49.
Fogolino, 115.
Francia, 27, 28, 30, 40.
Dresden, 28.

Gaddi, Agnolo, 7.
Gaddi, Taddeo, 4.
Ghiberti, 4.
Ghirlandajo, 9.
Giambono, Michele, 93.
London, Mr. L. Mond, 93.
Sir F. Leighton (formerly),
93.
Mr. Fairfax Murray, 93.
Dr. J. P. Richter, 93.
Venice, Academy, 93.
Museo Correr, 94.
St. Mark's, 93.
Salute, 94.
S. Trovaso, 94.
Giorgione, 31, 32, 71-89, 115,
136-147.
Bergamo, 77.

Giorgione, *continued.*
　Berlin, 84, 87, 88.
　Buda Pesth, 75, 82, 83, 84,
　　87, 143.
　Castalfranco, 80, 141.
　Dresden, 81, 88, 141.
　Florence, 76, 80, 81, 88, 134,
　　141.
　Hampton Court, 74, 88, 140-
　　146.
　London, Doetsch Collection
　　(dispersed), 82-84, 85.
　Lord Malmsbury, (137.)
　Madrid, 141.
　Milan, Signor B. Crespi, 84-
　　88.
　Paris, 81.
　St. Petersburg, 76.
　Venice Academy, 81, 88.
　　Seminario, 78, 79.
　Vienna, 144, 145.
Giotto, 4, 5, 6, 7, 14, 15.
Guercino, 21.
Guido Reni, 21.

Lanfranco, 21.
Lanzani, Polidoro.
　Glasgow, 91, 137.
　London, Lord Battersea, 91,
　　138.
　Mrs. R. Benson, 138.
　Sir William Farrer, 91, 137.
　Capt. Holford, 91, 138.
　Mr. A. H. Savage Landor,
　　145.
Leonardo, 10, 32, 89.
Licinio, 83, 85.
　London, Louisa Lady Ash-
　　burton, 83, 138.
　Capt. Holford, 138, 139.
　Milan, Casa Scotti, 138.
　Rome, Borghese, 138.
Lorenzetti, 15.
Lotto, 18, 36, 40.

Mantegna, 28, 29, 35, 40.
　Bergamo, 96.
　Berlin, 96.
　Dresden, 96.
　Dublin, 97.
　Florence, 97, 98.
　London, Louisa, Lady Ash-
　　burton, 95, 96.
　Mr. Charles Butler (99,
　　100).
　Mr. L. Mond, 96.
　National Gallery, 98 (99).
　Mr. J. E. Taylor (98).
　Tours, 98.
　Vienna, 98.
　Wilton House, Lord Pem-
　　broke, 97.
Marconi, Rocco, 126-128.
　Breslau, 126.
　London, Lord Ashburnham,
　　127.
　Mr. Charles Butler, 127.
　Mr. J. P. Carrington, 126.
　National Gallery, 128.
　Lord Northbrook, 126.
　Sir M. S. Stewart, 126.
Strasburg, 126, 127.
Venice, Academy, 127.
Masaccio, 4.
Mazzola, Filippo.
　London, Mr. G. Donaldson,
　　108.
　Lady Lindsay, 121.
Melozzo, 89.
Michelangelo, 10, 16, 17, 31,
　40, 45.
Michele da Verona.
　Mells Park, Frome, Mrs.
　　John Horner, 116, 120.
Montagna, Bartolommeo, 114-
　116.
　London, Sir W. Farrer, 114,
　　115, 116.
　Miss Hertz, 115.
　Sir B. Samuelson, 115.

Montagna, *continued.*
Milan, Poldi Pezzoli, 116.
Panshanger, Lord Cowper, 115.
Paris, The Louvre, 117.
Windsor, 116.

Orcagna, 7.

Palma, 36.
Palmezzano, 124.
Perugino, 9, 11.
Piazza, Calisto.
Lord Malmsbury, 92.
Piero dei Franceschi, 32, 40.
Pisanello, 93.
Pordenone, 143.
Predis, Ambrogio da, 121.
" Pseudo-Basaiti," 112.

Quirico da Murano.
Brescia?, 102.

Raphael, 9, 11, 20, 27, 40, 89.
London National Gallery, 27.
Rome, Vatican, 27.
Romanino.
Glasgow, 137.
London, Captain Holford, 91.
Rondinelli.
London, Louisa, Lady Ash-
burton, 123.
Captain Holford, 123.
Sir B. Samuelson, 124.
Rosso, 49.
Rubens, 80, 81.

Santacroce, Francesco, 135.
London, Mrs. R. Benson, 135.
Mr. Charles Butler, 135.
Santacroce, Girolamo, 108, 127.
Liverpool, 108.
London, Captain Holford, 91, 108.
Lord Northbrook, 108.

Santacroce, G., *continued.*
Mr. G. Salting, 108.
Milan, Poldi Pezzoli, 127.
Schiavone, Andrea.
London, Sir W. Farrer, 91.
Sir E. Burne-Jones, 137.
Sebastiani, Lazzaro, 105.
London, Mrs. B. W. Currie, 105.
Venice, Academy, 115.
Signorelli, 11, 16.
Simone Martini, 15.
Sodoma, 65.
Solario, 106.
Richmond, Sir F. Cook, 107.
Milan, Brera, 107.
Signor Crespi, 107.
Poldi Pezzoli, 107.
Speranza, 117, 118.
Brussells, M. Léon Somzée, 118.
Squarcione, 94.
Berlin, 95.

Tintoretto, 17, 45.
Titian, 40, 45, 80, 86, 87, 88, 90, 92, 104.
Brussells, M. Somzée (91).
Hampton Court (91).
London, Louisa, Lady Ash-
burton (91).
Mrs. R. Benson (91).
Lord Brownlow (91).
Lord Cowper (91).
Lord Malmsbury (91).
Mr. A. H. Savage Landor, (145).
Duke of Westminster (91).
Padua, Scuola del Santo, 86, 87.
Venice, Academy, 87.
Frari, 87.
Toschi, 21, 22.

Uccello, 4.

Velasquez, 82.
Veneto, Bartolommeo, 121, 135, 136.
  Bergamo, 135.
  Frankfort, 136.
  London, Mrs. R. Benson, 136.
  Milan, Ambrosiana, 136.
  Brussells, M. Léon Somzée, 136.
  Dresden, 136.
Veneziano, Domenico, 8.
Verrocchio, 32, 110.
Viti, Timoteo, 9, 27.
Vivarini, Alvise, 32, 40, 105, 106, 112, 113.
  London, Mrs. B. W. Currie, 105.
    National Gallery, 111.
    Mr. G. Salting, 105.

Vivarini, *continued*.
  Milan, Signor Bagati Valsecchi, 111.
  Paris, Comtesse de Béarn, 105.
  Venice, Academy, 111.
  Windsor, 105.
Vivarini, Antonio, 93, 94.
Vivarini, Bartolommeo, 99, 100, 101.
  London, Mr. Charles Butler (101).
    National Gallery, 99.
  Naples, 100.
  Oxford, Mr. McNeil Rushforth (101).

Zaganelli, 124.
Zevio, Stafano da, 93, 94.